MASTERCLASS

# MASTERCLASS

*Expert lessons in kitchen skills*

\*

CAROLINE CONRAN

PHILIPPA DAVENPORT

ELIZABETH DAVID

PRUDENCE LEITH

BARBARA MAHER

ANTON MOSIMANN

RICHARD OLNEY

ELISABETH LAMBERT ORTIZ

MARGARET PATERSON

ANNE WILLAN

*Jill Norman & Hobhouse Ltd*

First published 1982 by Jill Norman & Hobhouse Ltd
90 Great Russell Street, London WC1B 3PY

*British Library Cataloguing in Publication Data*

Maseterclass: expert lessons in kitchen skills
1. cookery
i. Norman, Jill
641.5     TX652.7

ISBN 0-906908-46-9
ISBN 0-906908-80-9 Pbk

Typeset by Inforum Ltd, Portsmouth
Printed and bound in Great Britain by
R. J. Acford Ltd., Industrial Estate, Chichester, Sussex

# Contents

# Introduction

This is a collection of essays on aspects of quite ordinary everyday cooking that seem to baffle many people.

'Have ready the nicely poached eggs' you may read in a recipe book, without so much as a hint about how to produce these well shaped, tidy objects. 'Over the years I think that I have received more pleas for advice on the technique of poaching eggs than on any other aspect of cookery' says Elizabeth David and her mail box has never been devoid of pleas for advice on the most diverse subjects.

'Meanwhile make the pastry' is another frustrating instruction, as is 'serve with mayonnaise' or 'roast the joint'. How do you accomplish these things – and what do you do when you try and things go wrong – when your sauce curdles, your soufflé fails to rise, your jam does not set? Why do different fats give different results, and is the one you always use necessarily the best for the particular dish you want to make?

On these and other similar matters, cooks often search desperately through all the wisdom accumulated on their kitchen shelf, but seldom find the answer in time to avert looming disaster. Many people lose interest, decide they can't make bread or pastry, are not good at soufflés or sponges.

In this book, ten experienced cooks remove the irritation and mystery from a number of these vexing problems. They explain in detail how and why processes work, give advice on previous mistakes and sometimes tell you what you can do to put things right. Each of them knows thoroughly and has a particular interest in the subject he or she has written about. This is evident from tell-tale phrases in their essays which betray fascination with the process described.

In roasting, says Richard Olney, 'the intimacy of the cook's involvement . . . is unlike any other cooking experience'. Despite the undisputed uses of modern blenders, Elizabeth David 'still takes pleasure in settling down to make this extraordinary sauce (mayonnaise) by the old method'. By contrast, Prue Leith extols preserving as 'the most satisfyingly scientific of all branches of cookery', while to Elizabeth Ortiz 'no cooking method is as versatile or rewarding as that of stewing'. Anne Willan has 'always been fascinated by soufflés', and Anton Mosimann acknowledges that a good chef 'is recognised by his sauces'.

To Caroline Conran's observation that 'the smell of bread baking is the best of all kitchen smells', Barbara Maher asserts that 'there is nothing more delicious than a freshly baked home-made sponge cake'.

Here, then, is a book by ten of the most knowledgeable cookery enthusiasts written both for serious cooks who want to improve their cooking from other people's experience, and for beginners who will have a head start by learning these daunting but basic skills and techniques right at the outset.

# Making Bread

## CAROLINE CONRAN

Like lighting a fire or planting seeds, making and baking a loaf seems to be a most natural and also a most satisfying thing, presumably related to some very old and primitive act of survival, and handed down as a ritual and necessity from mother to daughter over thousands and thousands of years.

The smell of bread baking is the best of all kitchen smells, and when the loaves are out on their racks, crackling as the crust cools, a puff of pride and pleasure rises with the scented steam of the loaves.

Making a good loaf is not difficult; all you need is good flour, yeast, salt and water. Although the process is open to endless variations, they all more or less follow this pattern. Dough likes a pleasantly warm and slightly humid atmosphere, such as a warm kitchen.

1. The yeast is mixed with warm water, and may be given a food to start it working – this can be sugar or flour – and put in a warm place. It starts to bubble.

2. The bubbling yeast mixture is added to a quantity of flour, some salt and enough warm water to make a soft, pliable dough. A short rest of two or three minutes at this point allows the flour to absorb the water, which makes the dough more manageable.

3. The dough is kneaded by hand or machine. With each movement the gluten is clumped and then stretched into finer and finer strands; you can see them in the dough as you push it and knead it. You can feel the dough becoming

smooth, tense and elastic.

4. The dough is covered traditionally with a light film of oil or fat and a damp cloth, today with a sheet of plastic film, so that it will not form a skin on the outside. It is left to rise in a warm place for a quick rise, in a cold place for a slow rise. It will double or treble in size, and ripen to a rounded, stretchy cushion of holes.

5. It can be knocked back (punched to release the gas) and kneaded a second and even a third time for a very good texture, and left to rise as before.

6. The dough is knocked back and cut into pieces. It is rested two or three minutes, then each piece is shaped or moulded. To do this, flatten the piece of dough and then 'wind it up' almost like a clockwork spring, to give it the tension it needs to rise well.

7. Each loaf or roll is put onto its baking sheet or into a buttered tin and 'proved'. It likes a moist atmosphere, so it is lightly covered. It regains its full tension, and just about doubles in size.

8. The loaf is often slashed or pricked at the last moment so that after it goes into the oven and starts to bake and harden on the outside, the slashes can open up and split still wider to allow the maximum expansion of the dough.

9. The loaf goes into a hot oven, the heat expands the gas in the dough, making it rise still further. A tray of water in the oven makes a steamy atmosphere which helps the bread to expand. The outside caramelises and browns to a crust. The heat kills the yeast. The heat is lowered to finish cooking the dough more gently.

10. The loaf is taken out when it sounds hollow when tapped underneath. It is cooled on a rack to allow steam to escape.

All timing is variable: it depends on the weather outside, the warmth of the kitchen, how fresh the yeast is, and how wet the dough is. It is much easier to work in a warm kitchen with very fresh yeast and with a slightly slack dough.

Patience is essential. When you look at your dough after an hour or two and see that it is still disappointingly small, don't give in and use it anyway, leave it a while and perhaps move it to a warmer spot. You will eventually see results. Warming the flour and the bowl slightly beforehand helps to speed things up if you want to be quick.

Quantities are somewhat variable too, as some flours, particularly wholemeal flours, absorb more water than others. The business of adding more water to a dough that is too dry is extremely tricky. The dough goes slimy and dull and feels unpleasant. It sometimes doesn't recover its proper silky, springy texture. On the other hand, if you have added more than enough water you can always sprinkle in more flour and then use plenty more on the board or table where you are kneading it, sprinkling on a bit at a time to stop it sticking. So it is wise always to keep some flour in reserve for this operation.

## Wheat flour

Wheat flour, which is the flour most commonly and successfully used for bread-making, is made from cleaned wheat grains. Like most cereals, the wheat grain consists of pericarp and testa which cover the endosperm and the germ or embryo. The germ, when it is sprouting, feeds on

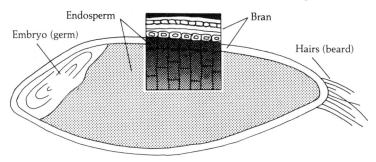

Diagrammatic longitudinal section of wheat grain.

the starchy endosperm. The germ contains the life of the seed, and the endosperm the bulk of the food. The scutellum, which lies between the germ and the endosperm, is rich in thiamin, and the germ contains a greater concentration of protein, oil and vitamin E than the rest of the grain; together scutellum and germ make up about 2–3% of the weight of the grain, so this is a small but important part. The remainder consists of the outer layers, including the aleurone layer, which make up the bran and constitute 12–15% of the grain, and the endosperm, which contains protein and the starchy material which goes into flour.

Flour for bread-making contains varying quantities of the grain and therefore varying quantities of the nutrients it provides. The different parts, once cooked, also have distinctly different flavours, the germ warm and nutty because of the oil it contains, the bran mealy and somewhat sackish because it contains quantities of fibre, and the endosperm more delicate, which is one reason why people through the ages have regarded white bread with the germ and bran removed as more suitable for elegant people to eat than rough, wholesome tasting brown or wholemeal bread. Whether you think they were misguided or not, it is now generally accepted that wholemeal bread with its high fibre content is better for the digestive system than white bread and that a lack of dietary fibre (present in bran) is amongst the most important direct causes of many of the so-called civilised diseases. I think a good choice of all different sorts of bread is the most agreeable.

What is not commonly known is that bran affects protein in the wheat and this makes it much more difficult to get a high rise on a wholemeal loaf than on a white one. At home this couldn't matter less, provided the loaf has a nice even texture, but for a commercial baker the good appearance of his loaf is a matter of economics – if it looks flat it won't sell. So he treats his wholemeal loaves to high temperatures and intense, high-speed mechanical mixing, and may add yeast-stimulating preparations, stabilisers, preservatives and so forth to make them look better. This is why it is difficult to buy a good commercial wholemeal loaf, unless it is baked by a dedicated baker (of which there is an increasing number) who knows what wholemeal bread should be like.

Wholemeal flour contains 100% of the grain, nothing added and nothing taken away, while white flour contains only about 72–76% of the grain, the parts taken away, germ and bran, being called offals and used mainly in animal foodstuffs. In modern steel roller mills brown flours, whose extraction rate lies somewhere between white flour and wholemeal, are made by adding a proportion of offals to white flour. As milling proceeds, the white flour and offals come off the machine in several different streams of varying fineness. A number of different flours (generally of about 80–90% extraction) can be made by mixing the white flour with one or other of the different available offal streams. So the composition, texture and flavour of brown flour can vary enormously even though the extraction rate does not. Stone-ground flour is more straightforwardly made, first ground and then sieved or bolted.

The quality of flour varies enormously, as you will find out when you start trying different brands at home. As well as differing in manufacturing methods and composition, it varies according to the quality of the wheat used. Most flours are in fact a mixture of different varieties, designed to give the required qualities necessary for baking a particular product such as bread.

**Types of flour**. The first thing to find out is the difference between the different types and grades of flour. As Elizabeth David says in her excellent book, *English Bread and Yeast Cooking* (Penguin Books, 1979), which is a must for every serious bread-maker, the different names used by different firms can be confusing, but basically bread flours are divided into four categories:

1. 100% wholemeal flour.

2. Wheatmeal flour which usually contains 80–90% of the whole grain. If this is not available use 4 cups of unbleached flour to 1 cup wholewheat.

3. Bleached white flour, which contains 72–76% of the whole wheat and has had practically all the bran and germ removed.

4. Unbleached white flour, which is of similar extraction but has a warm, creamy colour attributed to xanthophyll in the endosperm, and hasn't been treated by chemical bleaching. It tends to make a loaf with more charm and flavour than bleached white flour, but may not be so strong, so look for strong, unbleached white flour.

Some home-produced soft wheat is organically grown. If this is the case it will generally tell you on the flour packet.

**Gluten.** Gluten is the name by which the combination of the various proteins in flour is known. It is stretchy, elasticated stuff – if you chew a piece of uncooked bread dough you will find a stubborn sort of chewing gum develops between your teeth. This is the substance that traps the bubbles of carbon dioxide gas in the dough, giving the bread a good rise and elasticity (short, cake-like bread has its place too, but it is somehow much less satisfying than a good chewy loaf).

A rising dough must be brought to the point at which it is ripe, that is in the right springy condition to hold the gas produced by fermentation. If the dough is underripe then the gluten will not be elastic and will not stretch properly to hold the gas, but will split under the strain. In an overripe dough the elastic properties of gluten will be overstretched and weakened; the bubbles will burst and the structure of the dough will collapse or at best become coarse.

You can help strengthen the gluten by various means. It is toughened by all kinds of handling, punching, pummelling, kneading and mixing, by salt and by acidity from sour milk, buttermilk or lemon juice. It is also affected by various other ingredients that are used in your loaf, such as enzymes in yeast, fat, sugar, bran and wheatgerm, and the use of these ingredients will soften the texture of your loaf.

Once broken up, gluten loses its elasticity, so it is best to try and knead the dough smoothly without breaking its surface, and it is a good policy, when dividing the dough into loaves or into roll-sized pieces, to cut it with a knife rather than to pull it apart.

**Buying flour.** Wheats used for making bread are classified as hard or soft, according to their behaviour during milling, and strong or weak, according to their baking performance. These properties depend on climate, soil and the fertilisers used as well as on the variety of wheat. North American wheats almost all contain a large amount of strong protein and are hard, while English wheats are usually lower-protein soft wheats of weaker baking performance. A flour blend containing a larger quantity of North American wheats is usually a strong flour.

In general strong flours are best for bread-making, since they have the strength and resilience to form strong bubbles to trap the gas produced in the dough, giving the bread a good rise and elasticity. Good strong bread flour needs more time to mellow and become stretchy than weak flours such as are used for pastry and so forth. *The longer the bread-making process, the harder the flour needed and the less yeast must be added* since the enzymes in the yeast soften the gluten. A long fermentation takes several hours and the dough may even be left to ripen overnight. For a shorter process of half an hour to an hour or so, weaker flour is better as it ripens faster, and more yeast is needed to make it rise quickly.

As you will find, home-made short-process white bread does not keep well, has a coarser texture and often less flavour than long-process bread made with stronger flour and less yeast. It is, however, quite easy to make a very nice, nutty wholemeal loaf with weaker flour by a very shortened method – but eat it up quickly or it will go musty.

**How to choose the right brand of flour.** Fortunately there are many small flour-millers in England who are utterly dedicated to producing a really good product. Many use old watermills or windmills, some with stone millstones still at work. Try to track down flour milled by small, independent millers, whose livelihood depends on the quality and flavour of their flour and who really care. Their flours are to be found in high-class grocery shops and good health-food stores. Try the different brands and be sure to try any locally milled flour you can find.

**Additives.** Although a recent report suggests changes, flours other than wholemeal are required by law to be boosted or as the trade says 'enriched' with extra nutrients: calcium in the form of chalk, iron, thiamin and nicotinic acid.

White bread flour manufactured by any of the large millers is also likely to contain extra ingredients 'to improve palatability, crumb texture, colour and keeping qualities'. So may their brown flour (80–90% extraction). These additives may include bleaching and improving agents, nutrients, enzyme active preparations etc., etc.

Most bakers buy flour from the big millers, so if you buy flour from the baker it will make a loaf of bread all right, but it may be a rather characterless loaf even if it looks professional, which is the exact opposite of what one wants to achieve. At home, bread can look as lop-sided and crude as anything – all the better if it has plenty of character, as long as it tastes good.

**Keeping flour.** It seems paradoxical that while wholemeal flour should not be kept more than three to four months or six at the most, white flour improves with keeping; the longer it is kept once the bran and germ have been extracted, the more the baking quality is improved and the whiter it gets. To hasten this ageing and ripening process, bleaching agents are added to produce instant bleached white flour. Buy unbleached flour when you can find it for a nice, creamy loaf with a slightly nutty taste.

Wholemeal flour contains the wheatgerm oil which goes rancid if it is stored in the wrong conditions, such as a warm kitchen cupboard. It should be kept in a cool, dry, airy place. Buy wholemeal flour in smallish quantities to avoid the possibility of its going off. It develops a musty, acrid smell when it gets too old, so the fresher the better.

Another hazard with wholemeal flour is parasites – it is possible for the odd egg cluster to slip through with the flour since these are smaller than the particles of bran. In warmish conditions such as the hot, well-lit shelf of an ignorant grocer these can hatch and you may find yourself with a grub or even a moth in your flour. So buy flour from a reliable source with a quick turnover.

## Bakers' yeast – Saccharomyces cerevisiae

Fresh bakers' yeast is a sweet-smelling, pale beige, pasty substance which is commercially grown on specially selected molasses; it can be obtained in small bakers' shops and some grocers'. When very new, it holds together in a brittle block; as it gets old it tends to crumble into little pieces. Like all yeasts, it contains a microscopic, single-celled fungus which reproduces if it is fed and provided with warm, moist conditions, and it multiplies rapidly. So if you mix a piece of fresh yeast with a batter of warm water (35°C/95°F) and flour, it will start to multiply and feed, giving off carbon dioxide gas which causes the batter to ferment. Bakers call this fermenting batter the sponge.

Fresh yeast (in fact all yeast) can be killed by heat but not by cold – it can be kept covered in the refrigerator for several days, and in the freezer for several months. When defrosting frozen yeast use it up as soon as it is workable or it will rapidly deteriorate.

Dried active yeast, which usually comes in the form of granules, keeps indefinitely and is therefore a good standby. It is activated at a slightly higher temperature than fresh yeast (43°C/110°F) and according to the instructions on the packet needs sugar to start it going, although in fact it will start working, more slowly, with flour as a food. It is about twice as concentrated as fresh yeast, so use half as much by weight.

## Salt

'The bridle of the steed yeast', salt not only has a considerable effect on the flavour of bread but it checks fermentation, makes the gluten tougher and holds the rising to a slower but steadier process.

When making bread it is best not to let raw, undiluted salt come in contact with the yeast when making up dough, as this will bring its development almost to a standstill. One method of adding the salt is to dissolve it in the part of the liquid not used to dissolve the yeast; this is good for sea salt. Another is to make a well in the centre of the flour, sprinkle the salt around the top edge and pour the yeast and water into the well; this is a good method for table salt, the fine-grained variety.

The quantity of salt should be 15–45 g/½–1½ oz to every 1½ kg/3 lb of flour, according to taste and the type of bread being made. In a short-time loaf, salt should be used more sparingly than in a long-fermentation loaf. I always use sea salt, but not the kind that comes in hard round granules. I prefer either Malden salt crystals, which must be dissolved before use, or a delicious fine sea salt called La Baleine, but make certain that you get the fine one.

An Italian flat bread made with olive oil, called *focaccia*, which is served straight from the oven in Roman restaurants, has coarse salt scattered over the top of the dough just before it is baked. The hot, crackling salt crystals (Malden salt is ideal) give a lovely flavour to the bread, which should be eaten hot or warm. (If you try and keep it the salt attracts moisture and the top of the bread goes soggy.)

## Sugar and other yeast foods

To speed up fermentation various things can be added to feed the yeast. Sugar is one, but don't add too much or it will kill the yeast. Half a teaspoon of sugar helps to start the yeast working, although I often prefer to use a batter of flour and water, which gives a slower and steadier start. Instead of sugar you can use honey or molasses or even malt. Mashed potatoes or cooled potato water are good feeding for yeast, and soya flour also acts as an 'improver'. Vitamin C, ascorbic acid, is another improver which works by increasing the ability of the dough to hold gas. It is highly effective as I found out at a yeast-baking course at the Flour Advisory Bureau. We were set to making orange bread, which I snobbishly thought would not be my sort of thing, so I secretly left out the orange juice. I was then mortified to see everybody else's bread rising in graceful billows, while mine sat dull and sluggish in the bottom of the tin.

If using ascorbic acid tablets, which is an easy chemical way of speeding things up if you should need to so do, you will need half a tablet (25 mg) to 750 g/1½ lb cups flour.

## Liquids

Usually water, but you can use milk for a richer, softer loaf. An excess of liquid can give a poor crumb structure, a heavy loaf and, in the case of white bread, a grey colour.

## Fats and oils

These enrich the bread and help it to keep well. A bit of fat will help to give a short-time dough the ability to retain gas during baking, although a dough made by the long-fermentation method can do this without any fat.

Fat also affects the flavour, so use butter or very good lard rather than a dull vegetable shortening.

## Other flours

**Granary flour** is a sort of hybrid flour, containing pieces of malted grain which give a sweetness and stickiness in the baking. It is delicious if used mixed with either wholemeal or brown flour, and is apparently extremely healthy.

**Rye flour** with its distinctive flavour is not easy to use at home with any great results. It has no gluten to speak of, so it is best to mix it with other flours.

**Buckwheat flour, cornmeal, barleymeal, oatmeal and bean flour** can all be added to a basic dough in varying quantities to vary the flavour and texture. In hard times these rather coarse flours and meals were frequently used to make bread, but it was always *faute de mieux*, with the exception of cornmeal, which when cooked and mixed with wheat flour makes a nice yeast-bread.

## Kneading

Kneading dough is a rather long-winded business, and in spite of the poetic things people say about this – 'wonderfully relaxing and satisfying' and 'so good for releasing the aggressions' – it can actually be rather boring. It is, however, necessary; the movement of kneading forms the gluten into long strands which gradually strengthen and join up into a fine framework which will contain all the minute bubbles of carbon dioxide formed by the fermenting yeast.

You should knead smoothly and rhythmically, folding the mass of dough towards you and then pushing it smoothly down and away from you with the heels of your palms. Give it a little turn every few strokes and sprinkle a little extra flour under it if it seems to be sticking.

## Proving

Apparently a common fault of home bread-makers is

underproving their dough in the final stages – they are in too much of a hurry to get the thing into the oven and do not allow it to expand enough. I personally find that many people overprove their bread and end with a flat loaf of a coarse texture, which tastes stale before it even comes out of the oven. The rule of thumb is to allow the loaf, once shaped, to double in size. A freeform loaf or rolls will wobble on their tray when you shake them. The actual timing will vary according to whether you have a warm or a cold kitchen and can take from 15 to 40 minutes. To double-check, poke the dough lightly with your finger – if the dough is dryish and springs back immediately the loaves need a little longer, if it is sticky and fills out slowly they are ready, and if it doesn't spring back at all get them into the oven quickly or the texture will be spoiled.

If the whole thing has reached the top of the tin and gone flat and bubbly you can try a rescue operation by knocking it back and reshaping it, but you will not get a really good loaf as the flavour may be altered and the crumb structure will be coarse or collapse.

## Keeping bread

Bread is best kept at room temperature. It reacts badly to cold and therefore to being put in the refrigerator where it quickly becomes stale, but oddly enough it freezes extremely well – in fact it deteriorates less than practically any other frozen foodstuff. So if you want to make large quantities you can keep a supply of home-made bread quite successfully for a few days or even a month or two.

During freezing and subsequent thawing the bread stales to about the same extent as it would in 24 hours at normal temperature. However, if it is kept in the freezer over a longer period than a week or two, the crust tends to get dry and when the bread is thawed out it very disobligingly detaches itself from the crumb part in the middle.

## Simple breads

The simplest and most primitive form of bread is made with flour, water and salt, or even more simply with flour and water. This unleavened bread can be made and cooked without an oven, over a tiny fire – important when fuel and resources are scarce. In some country districts of India, Afghanistan and parts of the Middle East it is still the staple food. It is usually made by the women exactly as they have made it for several thousands of years, and it is eaten as soon as it is cooked, or dried, otherwise it loses its light texture and pleasant, nutty flavour.

The Indian chappati is a good example of unleavened bread made in the simplest way. It is handled and kneaded and patted and rested so that the gluten develops and the dough becomes quite elastic and can be formed into flat rounds which are cooked on a hot iron plate called a *tawa* in a few minutes. (You can use a heavy iron frying pan or griddle to cook them.) The Indian cook does everything by his or her senses – the dough will feel right when it is right; there is no measuring except by eye. The bread, once cooked, is used as a scoop to help eat the food which accompanies it.

## Chappatis

| 225 g | 8 oz | chappati flour (atta) or 81% brown flour |
|---|---|---|
| ½ tsp salt | | |
| 100–170 ml | 4–6 fl oz | lukewarm water |
| Makes 12 chappatis | | |

Mix the flour and salt together in a bowl. Add the water. If the dough is too wet and sticky to handle, add more flour; if it is too dry sprinkle drops of water into it until it is soft, malleable and cohesive and does not stick to your hands. It should be as soft and moist as possible without being sticky. Knead it well on a lightly floured board and continue kneading until it feels supple (about 5 minutes should be enough). Form into a ball, cover with a wet cloth and leave for an hour for the gluten to develop.

Knead the dough again for 5 minutes. The dough becomes silky and much more stretchy and elastic. It will have a more satisfying chewy texture than if it was not kneaded. Divide the dough into 12 portions and shape each into a little ball. Roll each piece out into a thin disc, using plenty of dry flour to prevent it sticking. Heat the frying pan or griddle over a medium heat. When it is hot, put the chappatis onto the hot metal and as soon as the first bubbles appear turn them over. When they seem to be cooked and have lost their transparent look remove them from the pan.

When all the chappatis are cooked hold them briefly over a hot gas flame or hotplate until they puff up. (The steam inside forces the top and bottom of the chappatis apart.) Serve in a folded napkin and eat at once.

As you must cook them at the last moment, it is quite exhausting trying to make them for several people. My way out is to make 4 large chappatis instead of 12 small ones, and let people tear bits off them as they like. (An Indian mother with a large family may take all morning making enough chappatis for lunch!)

Related to chappatis, but closer to the bread we know in the West, are the leavened flat breads eaten widely in the Middle East and North India. They were originally made with a sourdough leaven, but today fresh yeast is often used. The flour used is usually somewhat refined or white and the bread is cooked in a flat shape either in a pit oven or on hot stones.

*Markouk* bread, also known as *tannour*, from the Lebanon, Syria and Iraq, is wafer-thin and about one metre across. It is made with a sourdough leaven and shaped by a special kneading process known only to the mountain women. It is cooked on a large, convex griddle over a small fire. Once cooked it can be folded like a hankie for travelling. It can then be rolled round a filling of herbs and spices to make a sort of sandwich.

Another fairly primitive bread is *khubz kamaj*, a flat, disc-shaped bread. This simple recipe is excellent for getting the feel of bread dough; it rises rapidly and in a most encouraging way, and even children can make it with no trouble. If eaten straight away it is excellent – in fact one just can't stop eating it. Use a soft flour (that is an ordinary plain flour) for this recipe as the fermentation is rapid owing to the large quantity of yeast and sugar to feed the yeast. I find I can also use this dough for making pizza.

## Khubz

| | | |
|---|---|---|
| 1 tsp salt | | |
| 340 g | 12 oz | plain flour – the sort used for making cakes etc. |
| 1 tbs fresh yeast or ½ tbs dried | | |
| 1 level tbs sugar | | |
| 250 ml | about 8 fl oz | warm water |

Mix the salt into the flour in a large bowl. Mix the yeast with the sugar in half the water. Stir until all the ingredients are dissolved and leave in a warm place for 15 minutes. Add to the flour with the rest of the water kneading thoroughly until you have a smooth dough. Allow it to rest while you wash the bowl, then knead lightly on a floured board for a few minutes. Replace in the bowl, cover with plastic film and allow to rise in a warm place until well risen to more than double the original size. It should take 45–60 minutes. Roll out ½ cm/¼ inch thick on a breadboard sprinkled with flour. Make into one large round or cut out several small ones with a saucer. Place on a greased baking tray, prick the top here and there with a fork, and prove for 15 minutes, covered. Bake in a moderate oven, gas 5/190°C/375°F for 30 minutes until golden. Brush the top with melted butter and serve while still warm.

Another example of a quickly made bread is Doris Grant's nutty, dark, wholesome loaf, made with wholemeal flour. Again plenty of yeast and sugar are added and the dough, after mixing, is put straight into the tins to cut fermentation time. If it was given the usual double fermentation the dough, which is scarcely kneaded and rather well fed, would quickly get overripe, lose any elasticity it had and collapse.

Although it takes hardly any time to make, this loaf is delicious, but like all short-fermentation breads does not keep for more than a day or two, so make it in small quantities or freeze it.

## *Doris Grant's loaf*

| | | |
|---|---|---|
| 300–350 ml | 10–12 fl oz | hand-hot water |
| 4 tsp Barbados or dark brown sugar | | |
| 2 tsp dried yeast or 4 tsp fresh | | |
| 450 g | 1 lb | wholewheat flour |
| 2 tsp salt | | |

Butter the bread tin or tins. Put a third of the water into a measuring cup or jug and stir in $\frac{1}{2}$ teaspoon of the sugar and the yeast. Leave on one side for 10 minutes to froth up. Put the flour into a large bowl and mix in the remaining sugar and the salt. Add the frothy yeast and the remaining water to the flour and mix well to a dough. Wholemeal flour absorbs a little more water than white flour and this dough is meant to be rather wet and softer than ordinary bread dough. Squeeze and knead the dough with your hands for a few minutes – it will become smoother and less sticky – and then put the dough into the tin or tins. Cover with a cloth or place the tins in a large plastic bag and leave for 45–60 minutes, until the loaves have doubled in size. When the dough is nearly ready, pre-heat the oven to gas 6/ 200°C/400°F. Bake a large loaf for 35–40 minutes, or two small ones for 25–30 minutes. Remove the loaves from the tins and cool on a wire rack.

Do not let it rise for too long. If you go away and forget this bread while it is rising, it will reach the top of the tin and then pass the moment when it is ready to go in the oven. As it continues to ferment the bubbles will get coarser and start collapsing so that the finished loaf will not have a good texture (structure) but will be somewhat coarse, dry and crumbly, and will go stale even more quickly than usual.

In contrast to the short methods given above, the following white loaf is made with strong bread flour, a small quantity of yeast and no sugar by the longer method. It is a very good basic loaf, and by perfecting the making of it you will learn how to handle dough. For example if you want to speed it up a bit, you can slightly heat the bowl or the flour or both before you start, and keep it rising in a warm place. If you wish to go out or slow down the bread for some reason, you can put it in a cooler place, even a cold larder or refrigerator where it will sit happily all night. It takes some time to recover from the refrigerator, however, so don't expect instant breakfast rolls – you must give it time to pick up again in a warm atmosphere before you shape it.

## White bread

| 900 g–1 kg | 2 lb plus a few handfuls | plain white strong flour |
|---|---|---|
| 15 g | $\frac{1}{2}$ oz | fresh yeast |
| 600 ml | 1 ping and 3–4 tbs | hot water |
| 2–3 tsp salt | | |
| 1 tbs olive oil | | |
| handful of cornmeal (not cornflour) | | |

Put the flour in a warm bowl. Mix yeast with 3–4 tablespoons warm water and pour into a well in the centre of the flour, mixing in a bit of the surrounding flour with a spoon as you do so, and scatter a bit of flour over the top – this will feed the yeast and start it working. It takes a little longer than sugar but is a very old and good way.

Sprinkle the salt round the edge of the well. Leave in a warm place until the flour on the yeast pool starts to crack and the yeast to froth and bubble. Pour in most of the remaining water and mix quickly to a rough dough. If it's too dry add more water, it too wet add a little more flour but keep it on the slack side. Leave to rest while you wash the bowl.

Knead the dough on a floured board with floured hands, sprinkling on more flour as necessary. It should feel loose, silky and resilient. After 5–10 minutes' kneading put dough in a clean warm bowl with 1 tablespoon olive oil to coat it all over to stop it drying out. Cover with plastic film and leave to rise in a moderately cool place for up to 3 hours. You can leave out the oil but it actually helps the flavour of the bread.

When risen to three to four times its size, knock down thoroughly, cut the dough in half and form two loaves. Use greased tins or make round freeform loaves, but make sure they are taut and plump or they won't rise well. Dust the tops with flour. Put freeform loaves on a baking sheet scattered with cornmeal, cover the loaves loosely and leave to prove for 20–30 minutes or until well risen and taut. Heat oven to gas 7/220° C/425° F. Smother the tops with flour, put the loaves in the oven – you can slash the tops with a very sharp knife if you like, sprinkling the cuts with drops of water. Turn the heat down to gas 4/180° C/350° F after 20 minutes. Bake for 40–45 minutes in all. Cool on racks.

You can substitute 4–5 tablespoons of milk for some of the warm water, and use melted butter to coat the inside of the bowl instead of oil.

One of the things frequently wrong with home-made white bread is that it doesn't have the satisfying chewiness of a good loaf such as a cottage loaf bought from a really good baker. The following recipe which includes potatoes gives a very delicious, substantial loaf, not heavy but with a good springy, elastic texture. This is a Balkan recipe, but mashed potatoes were often included in old-fashioned bread recipes. In *The Cook and Housewife's Manual*, written under the name of Meg Dodds (whose real name was Isobel Johnstone) in 1826, the yeast leaven or sponge for the dough is made by mixing pea flour, rye flour, mashed potatoes and wheat flour with sugar, water and fresh yeast, or, more simply, mealy mashed potatoes, brown sugar and fresh yeast.

## *A white loaf with mashed potatoes*

| | | |
|---|---|---|
| 30 g | 1 oz | *fresh yeast* |
| 550 ml | 18 fl oz | *warm water* |
| 900 g | 2 lb | *strong white bread flour* |
| 1½ tbs salt | | |
| 3 mealy boiled potatoes, mashed (175 g/6 oz ofter cooking) | | |
| 1 tbs fine cornmeal (not cornflour – cornmeal is like golden sand) | | |

Mix the yeast with 3 tablespoons of the measured water and 3 tablespoons of flour to make a thickish batter. Let it rise and froth in a warm place for half an hour.

Put the flour in a warm bowl, make a well in the centre, sprinkle salt round the edge, and put the yeast mixture, mashed potatoes and most of the water in the centre. Mix to a dough. It will be somewhat sticky, so use frequent but small sprinklings of flour on the work top or table while you knead the dough for 10 minutes. Then wash the bowl, put in the smooth and well kneaded dough, and cover with plastic film stretched across the top of the bowl. Leave to rise for several hours until billowing into a rounded mass and three times its original size. Large bubbles may appear – do not worry.

Knead the dough again briefly and cut it in half. Shape each half into a round, flatten it and then drawn in the sides to make a good round shape – this drawing-in gives tension to the loaf which helps it to rise well. Place on a baking sheet sprinkled with fine cornmeal. Sprinkle tops thickly with flour and cover lightly. Leave to prove for 15–20 minutes or a little more on a cold day. Meanwhile pre-heat oven to gas 7/220°C/425°F. When the loaves have proved and are swollen and tense, slash each with 3 parallel slashes. Allow to recover for 2 or 3 minutes, then place in the middle of the oven. After 15–20 minutes or so, when the loaves are well risen and the crust starting to turn golden, turn down the heat to gas 4/180°C/350°F and cook for a further 30–35 minutes until they sound hollow when tapped. Cool on racks.

A liberal dusting of flour on top of a loaf helps to protect the top crust; as well as preventing it from burning it lets it expand before the heat penetrates this insulating layer. The slashes also enable the loaf to expand evenly, as does the cornmeal on the tin – the bottom of the loaf can just slide across the tin as it expands widthways. In addition to this, the baked cornmeal on the bottom and the floury top give the loaf a beautiful appearance.

Another attractive thing about this loaf and other freeform white loaves is that the crust crackles and cracks as it cools, breathing out a delicious, appetising steam. This crackled, deep golden crust is a real triumph of bread-making and tastes superb.

This loaf keeps well. You can add caraway seeds, or colour and flavour it with saffron.

If you want to make a really fine wholemeal loaf with good keeping qualities then you will prefer the long-fermentation method. A loaf like the one below takes several hours to make, but most of this time it will be quietly rising by itself; you don't have to stand over it. It will keep up to a week without going musty, helped by the oil and honey.

## A wholemeal loaf

| | | |
|---|---|---|
| 30 g | 1 oz | *fresh yeast* or |
| 15 g | ½ oz | *dried yeast* |
| 600 ml | 1 pint | *warm water* |
| 900–1125 g | 2–2½ lb | *wholemeal flour* |
| 2–3 tsp salt | | |
| 2 tbs liquid honey | | |
| 2 tbs olive or sunflower oil | | |
| 2 tbs wheatgerm (optional) | | |
| 2–3 tbs raw resame seeds | | |
| Makes three 500 g/1 lb tin loaves | | |

Dissolve the yeast in half a cup of the measured amount of water, and stir in 2 or 3 tablespoons of flour. Leave in a warm place to start working. Measure 900 g/2 lb of flour into a large warm bowl. I like to use 3 parts fine wholemeal to 1 of coarse-ground.

Make a well in the centre and pour in the yeast. Dissolve the salt and honey in the warm water and add the oil. Pour it into the well in the flour, add the wheatgerm if you are using it, and mix it in with a wooden spoon at first and then with your hands.

When you have a mass of dough, evenly mixed, turn it out onto a floured table or working top. Let it rest while you wash the bowl and your hands and then knead the dough well for up to 10 minutes, sprinkling a little more flour over the working surface as it gets absorbed. The more you knead, the more you develop the gluten and the more stretchy, malleable and springy the dough becomes. You may need to add quite a considerable amount of flour during the kneading process if the dough is sticky – don't worry it will all be absorbed quite happily – it isn't like

pastry where adding more flour will make it stodgy and heavy. Put it back in the cleaned bowl, cover with plastic film and leave to rise for two or three hours, in a not too warm place.

When it has risen to at least double its original size, knock back the dough, put it onto a board and knead again briefly. Cut it into three, let it rest 2 or 3 minutes, then shape three tin loaves by rolling each piece into a ball, flattening the ball into a flat round, rolling up the round like a swiss roll rolling it in sesame seeds and then tucking the ends under. Drop each into a well buttered loaf tin, and push down lightly round the sides, giving a nice rounded top. Cover with a loose layer of plastic film and leave to prove until the loaf has risen well to the top of the tin. Meanwhile heat the oven to gas 7/220°C/425°F.

Put loaves into the hot oven, after 15 minutes turn down the heat to gas 4/180°C/350°F and cook for a further 25 minutes. Remove a loaf, tap the bottom to see if it is done, if it sounds hollow remove it, if not put it back for 5–10 minutes more. Cooking times are never exactly the same as ovens vary. Cool the loaves on a rack.

# Shortcrust Pastry

## PHILIPPA DAVENPORT

Shortcrust pastry is amazingly useful, the backbone recipe for so many good and inexpensive dishes. Yet pastry-making is an area of cookery which daunts lots of people, including many otherwise competent cooks.

The old adage about icy cold hands and a marble pastry slab being pre-requisites to good pastry-making is decidedly intimidating to anyone who owns neither – and if you feel thus doomed to failure at the outset your chances of success are inevitably reduced. It can also be discouraging when cookery books simply say 'make the pastry', as if pastry-making know-how were instinctive or inherited.

I used to be very nervous of pastry-making and avoided it for years, but I learned that pastry-making is not a gift you are either born with or without; it is a skill which can be acquired with a little guidance and practice – and I speak as one who has naturally warm hands and no marble, slate or other really cold work surface in the kitchen.

### Basic shortcrust

As the name indicates, shortcrust should be 'short', that is crisp, but not hard or tough, and melt-in-the-mouth but not over-rich. The basic ingredients are few: flour, fat, salt and water.

The flour is always plain, never self-raising, usually white. Brown pastry is made with wholewheat flour: this gives an interesting nutty flavour, but is more difficult to roll out and makes a rather heavy pastry if used alone. I suggest using half wholewheat and half white flour for brown pastry.

The best fat for well-flavoured pastry is butter. A cheaper mixture of half butter and half lard is also good for savoury pastry; lard shortens the texture, while butter gives fine flavour. Margarine doesn't contribute much to flavour or texture: I rate it as an economy measure to avoid.

Trying to guess weights is always hazardous, and an incorrect balance of ingredients is a common source of trouble with pastry-making. Too much fat gives an over-rich and crumbly shortcrust; too much flour makes it dry and hard; too much water makes the pastry tough and liable to shrink; on the other hand, too little water makes an unmanageable dough.

Use accurate scales and a set of standard kitchen measuring spoons (table cutlery varies too much in size) to ensure correct proportions. These are twice as much flour as fat, a pinch of salt for flavour, and what is usually described rather loosely as 'enough water to bind'. Different types and brands of flour have different rates of absorbency, so it is impossible to be absolutely precise about the amount of liquid needed, but on average you will need 1 teaspoon cold water for every 30 g/1 oz white flour used, marginally more for brown flour.

To make 250 g/$\frac{1}{2}$ lb basic shortcrust pastry you will need:

| 250 g | $\frac{1}{2}$ lb | *plain white flour —or half wholewheat flour and half white flour* |
|---|---|---|
| a pinch of salt | | |
| 2 tsp caster sugar | | |
| 125 g | $\frac{1}{4}$ lb | *butter or half each butter and lard* |
| about 8 tsp cold water | | |

It is worth noting that, when a recipe calls for, say, 250 g/$\frac{1}{2}$ lb pastry, this refers to the weight of flour used to make the pastry, not the total weight of all the ingredients.

## Sweet shortcrust

Although basic shortcrust can, of course, be used for sweet dishes as well as for savoury ones, sweet shortcrust makes sweet pastry dishes taste better. Ingredients and method are almost the same as for basic shortcrust, but sugar is added to sweeten the pastry, and the mixture is slightly enriched in two ways: the fat is always butter (never half butter half lard), and egg yolk replaces most of the water used to bind the dough. The sugar must be caster sugar – granulated is too coarse-grained.

To make 250 g/½ lb sweet shortcrust you will need:

| | | |
|---|---|---|
| *250 g* | *½ lb* | *plain white flour – or half wholewheat flour and half white flour* |
| *a pinch of salt* | | |
| *2 tsp caster sugar* | | |
| *125 g* | *¼ lb* | *butter* |
| *1 small egg yolk mixed with about 2 tsp cold water* | | |

## Making the dough

The traditional method of making the pastry by hand is not as difficult in practice as you may at first fear. You can feel confident that your first batch of shortcrust will be edible, if not perfect, and you can expect to become proficient after two or three attempts.

Take the fat out of the fridge about 30 minutes before starting to make the pastry so it will soften a little. If rock hard, the fat will not blend well and this can cause blistered pastry. If too soft, it will be messy to handle and produce oily results.

Choose a large mixing bowl and sieve the flour and salt (and sugar if making sweet shortcrust) into it. Hold the sieve high as you shake it to aerate the ingredients well. If using brown flour, then tip any bran remaining in the sieve into the bowl.

Add the fat to the bowl and cut it up with a palette knife, or any other round-bladed knife, until each piece is no larger than a pea. I used to think it would save time and effort to cut up the fat first, but cutting it up in the bowl is far more effective because each time you cut, new surfaces of fat get coated with flour.

Now for what is called 'rubbing in', a misnomer if ever I heard one. The aim is, of course, to get flour and fat well blended, but if you literally rub the fat into the flour everything becomes a horrid oily mess and sticks to your fingers. Whether your hands are warm or cold is of relatively little importance. What does matter is that you should use your hands *lightly*. Pick up a small amount of the ingredients in each hand, raise your hands well above the bowl, then *gently* run your thumbs across your fingertips, from the smallest to the forefinger, two or three times: the ingredients will sift and trickle through your hands back into the bowl. Nothing appears to have happened, the texture of the ingredients still looks the same. Persevere. Repeat these actions over and over, lightly and steadily, stopping occasionally to shake or tap the bowl to make any lumps come to the surface so you will pick them up. A pleasing rhythm develops as you acquire the knack. Your wrists may begin to ache, they are doing most of the work; your fingers are not using pressure, just stroking lightly.

After 6 minutes or so the mixture, magically, no longer looks like flour speckled with lumps of fat, more like a bowl of uniformly ground almonds or breadcrumbs. When this stage is reached it is time to stop (not earlier, for if flour particles are not evenly coated with fat they will absorb an unnecessary quantity of liquid).

Liquid is now needed to bind the ingredients to a dough. The liquid should be very cold to counteract the warmth your hands will have imparted to the fat and flour. To minimise the chances of using too much, it should be added very gradually and carefully blended in after each addition; it is all too easy for a beginner to add too much (which makes tough, heavy pastry).

First sprinkle on 3 teaspoons of water (or egg yolk mixed with water for sweet shortcrust) and stir it in well with the palette knife. Then sprinkle on and stir in 2 teaspoons: the mixture will begin to cling together. Now sprinkle on the same amount again, but this time use the flat of the knife blade to press the mixture together: it will form into fairly large lumps. Begin to draw and press the dough together lightly with your fingers; it should feel pliable, a little moist but not tacky, and will come away cleanly from the sides of the bowl to make a ball quite readily if it contains enough liquid. You may have to work in a little more liquid to get the right consistency (the knack of judging when consistency is right takes a little practice), but go very cautiously at this stage – just a drop or two looks ridiculously little when you add it but, once absorbed, it can make a surprisingly big difference to the consistency of the dough.

Turn the ball of dough onto a flat, unfloured work surface. Delicately draw the outer edges of the dough into the centre with your fingertips. Continue kneading it like this for a minute or so until smooth and free from cracks. Wrap the ball of dough in a sheet of clingfilm to prevent the surface drying out, and refrigerate it for 20–30 minutes so that it recovers from handling.

## Using a food mixer or processor

Making shortcrust pastry in a food mixer or processor is, of course, far quicker than making it by hand and, speed apart, people who worry about their skill in 'rubbing in' often prefer to use a machine. The potential danger of making pastry by machine is over-working the dough: everything happens so quickly and the mixture can easily become very oily. The warmth generated by a machine is considerable: counteract this by using fat straight from the fridge so it is really cold when blended into the flour, and use all butter (even when very cold, lard is too soft-textured). Use less fat (three quarters the amount used for making pastry by hand) and less water (about two thirds).

Put the sifted flour and salt into the bowl (together with sugar if making sweet shortcrust). Dice the butter with a knife *before* adding it to the bowl. Turn the machine on, and switch it off again as soon as the 'ground almond stage' is reached – this can take as little as 10 seconds with some models. With the machine running, add a little liquid and stop as soon as the dough is bound together – again this seems to happen with the speed of lightning. Knead and chill the dough as described for making shortcrust by hand.

## Rolling out the pastry

Take the chilled ball of dough out of the fridge and place it on a lightly floured work surface (if heavily floured you could alter the proportions of the pastry ingredients). The pastry will be too hard to shape straight away without cracking, so leave it for 10 minutes at room temperature to soften a little. Increase the waiting time to 15 minutes if the pastry has been refrigerated for longer than half an hour, considerably more if it has been chilled overnight.

The less pastry is handled (touched or rolled) the lighter and better it will be, so the aim is to roll it to the correct size and shape first go. Don't aim for a precise fit, but err marginally on the large side. Excess can always be trimmed away but, if the pastry is too small, you may be tempted to stretch it to fit and that is never successful: it may tear and will certainly shrink back again during baking. Alternatively you will have to re-roll it, which makes the pastry tougher.

Place the mould – the tin you are going to line, or the pie dish you are going to cover – beside you as a guide to size and shape. Mentally increase the diameter of the top to allow for depth and/or for a strip of pastry to go round the rim, then increase the diameter *again* by an extra, say, $\frac{1}{2}$ cm/ $\frac{1}{4}$ inch all round to allow for miscalculation and trimming. Dust your hand and a rolling pin with a little flour. Slightly flatten the dough with the palm of your hand to make a disc; if using an oval pie dish then ease the pastry into an oval shape with your hands.

A long wooden rolling pin is preferable to a short one, and a handleless version is best (handles encourage you to grip them, and a gripped pin produces short bursts of rolling, plus the danger of digging your knuckles into the dough). Place the rolling pin across the edge of the pastry nearest to you, and lay your hands flat on the pin spacing them well apart. Using light, even pressure, push *gently* with your hands to roll the pin away from you across the full width of the pastry in one continuous movement. Do this just once, then carefully lift the pastry and give it a clockwise quarter turn before rolling the pin across it again, in the same way and in the same direction as before. The point of turning the pastry between each rolling is 'to spread the load': everyone uses slightly more pressure with one hand than the other and random rolling invariably reflects this, producing pastry of ragged shape with some thick patches and possible tears in thin areas where the pastry has been over-stretched. A few long, gentle strokes with the pin will shape the pastry much more quickly, evenly and efficiently. If at any stage the pastry should stick to the pin, stop rolling immediately – going on might flake off a large layer of the pastry and/or cause a crack or tear. Scrape the pin clean and dust it, rather than the pastry, with a little more flour before continuing.

When the pastry is the shape, size and thickness you want it, transfer it to the tin or dish. There is no need to grease the tin except for tartlets. To avoid tearing it or distorting its shape in the process, put the rolling pin on one side of the pastry and roll it, wrapping the dough lightly round the pin as you do so. Lift the pin, position it into or over the centre of your chosen tin or dish, and unroll carefully.

## Flans, quiches and tarts

Fluted white china flan or quiche dishes look pretty, but they are best left to cookery book illustrators. From a cooking and eating point of view a metal fluted tin is far better. Metal conducts heat better than china, and a tin with a removable base is most practical of all – the sides can be slipped off after cooking which makes for easy unmoulding, slicing and serving.

Unroll the pastry as you lower it carefully into the tin. Using your fingers or a tiny ball of surplus dough, gently press the pastry onto the base of the tin, working gradually from the centre outwards, into the corners, then up the sides of the tin. Bend the surplus pastry over the rim and *either* cut it off by rolling the pin across the top of the tin, then neaten the pastry edge, pressing lightly round the rim with thumb and forefinger, *or* trim away excess with scissors about $\frac{1}{2}$ cm/$\frac{1}{4}$ inch beyond the rim. In the latter case, fold the surplus pastry back on itself and tuck it between the flutes of the tin and the walls of the pastry shell, then press the double-thick pastry against the sides of the tin. I prefer this method. It strengthens the walls of the pastry shell and this reduces the chances of their crumbling. It also means that the rim (the most exposed part of the pastry) is less likely to get too brown before the filling is cooked.

Prick the base of the pastry shell with a fork to release any air trapped underneath – this is to stop the base bubbling up during baking. The holes will close up during cooking so don't worry about the possibility of the filling leaking out. Then chill the pastry for another 5 minutes before filling and baking, to allow it to recover from handling. There is no need to cover it.

## Open plate tarts

Pie plates are baking tins that look like soup plates, round and shallow with a wide rim. They are measured by diameter from rim to rim. The rim provides a ledge on which to seal the pastry and so prevent it slipping back into the bowl of the dish. The rim also gives you an area to decorate.

Unroll the pastry and press it gently onto the base and up the sides of the tin as described for flans and tarts. Trim excess pastry with scissors to about $\frac{1}{2}$ cm/$\frac{1}{4}$ inch beyond the rim, then use thumb and forefinger to fold the extended edge under the main pastry rim to make a double-thickness rounded pastry edge that lies flush with the rim of the pie plate. Press the folded pastry lightly against the rim with your fingers and seal securely by decorating in one of the following simple ways.

**Fork pattern:** press the back of the prongs of a fork all the way round the rim of the pastry.

**Daisy pattern:** use the handle of a teaspoon in exactly the same way.

**Goffered:** slip the blunt edge of a knife under the pastry at intervals and lift it slightly while pressing the pastry on either side with index finger and thumb.

Prick the pastry base with a fork and chill for 5 minutes before adding the filling and baking.

## Single-crust pies

Pie dishes are usually round or oval – round ones traditionally being used for sweet pies, oval ones for savoury pies. They are deeper than pie plates and the rim is narrower, but it must be broad enough to seal the pastry properly, otherwise the pastry might lose its grip and slip.

In single-crust pies, pastry is used as a lid to cover the filling. The only contact between pastry and dish is on the rim, so whether the dish is metal or china has little effect on how the pastry cooks. (Do not, however, make a single crust fruit pie in a metal dish unless it has an enamelled finish: plain tin taints fruit.)

**Fillings.** Shortcrust pastry should never be cooked for longer than an hour, a point to bear in mind when choosing pie fillings.

Fruit is a popular candidate because it will cook from raw well within the time limit, and it provides a juicy contrast to crisp shortcrust. Sprinkle sugar between fruit layers, but not over the top layer of fruit or the pastry lid may absorb the sugar as it melts and so become soft and sticky.

Because of the time factor, when raw meat is used it must be high quality and cut into very small pieces. Larger chunks of tougher meat can also be used of course, but they must be partially cooked in advance and completely cooled before the pastry lid is placed on top. The cooling is essential. My insistence on this point is as a result of disasters occurring when I have used hot fillings: steam rises, soaks into the pastry and prevents it from cooking properly. At best the underside tastes raw, at worst it collapses into the dish.

**Making the lid.** Roll out the pastry to the shape of the dish, making it at least 4 cm/$1\frac{1}{2}$ inches larger in diameter. Cut from the perimeter a strip of pastry equal to the width of the rim of the dish. Damp the rim of the dish with a little water, press the pastry strip lightly onto it, then brush the top of the pastry strip with a little water.

Pile the cold filling into the dish, and mound it in the centre to support the pastry lid. If the filling is very soft or liquid, stand an upturned egg-cup in the centre of the dish and use its flat bottom to support the pastry.

Carefully lift the pastry lid, centre it over the filled pie dish, and unroll it so it covers the filling. At this stage the lid should be larger than the dish and overhang it slightly. Press lightly with your fingers to seal the two pastry rims together. Then lift the dish in one hand and take a sharp knife in the other. Hold the knife upright and at an angle so that the blade points away from the dish, and trim away excess pastry. Cutting from underneath like this gives a pastry edge marginally wider than the rim of the dish and allows for slight natural shrinkage of the pastry during cooking.

**Knocking up & fluting.** These curious sounding activities are simply a means of simultaneously sealing and decorating the pastry rim. To knock up, hold the blunt edge of a knife horizontally against the pastry edge and tap two or three times while pressing with the forefinger of your other hand against the inner rim of the pastry. This both presses the two layers of pastry together, and fans them out. To flute, hold the knife blade vertically and mark the knocked-up edge at intervals by drawing the blade lightly against the pastry.

**Glazing & decorating.** To give pastry lids a good finish they are usually glazed before baking, that is they are lightly brushed with liquid which turns to an appetising shine during baking. Lightly beaten egg (mixed with a drop of water and a little salt if you wish) gives a glossy golden finish to savoury pies; egg white used alone gives a very shiny look to sweet pies – for extra-crisp results a little sugar can be sprinkled on top. Milk is cheaper than egg and can be used to give a pleasant golden-brown finish to sweet and savoury pies.

Elaborate individual decorations were used to distinguish one pie from another in bygone times when domestic ovens were a rarity and it was common practice for housewives to take their pies to the local baker for cooking. Such decorations are, of course, unnecessary today but they are still fun to do and there is something satisfying about using up every scrap of the pastry you have made.

Lightly re-roll the trimmings and cut out leaf shapes or any other simple shapes with a sharp knife dipped in flour.

Cut decisively to avoid stretching and tearing the pastry. Press the decorations lightly onto the glazed pie – the glaze will act as a glue – then brush the top of the decorations with more glaze.

To allow steam to escape from the filling as it is created during cooking, make a couple of small slits in the pastry lid with the tip of a knife. Always do this *after* glazing or the glaze could seal up the slits.

## Double-crust pies

Double-crust pies consist of a filling sandwiched between two sheets of pastry. They are usually quite deep so the proportion of pastry to filling is not too heavy. They can be made in baking tins and dishes of various sorts, but pie dishes are most frequently used for large pies, and tartlet tins for individual pies.

If using a pie dish, divide the pastry into two pieces, making one slightly larger than the other. Use the larger piece to line the dish as described for flans and pie plates, but do *not* double the pastry at the rim (because the doubling effect will be achieved by the addition of the pastry lid). Simply let the surplus pastry hang over the edge of the dish and brush the pastry on the rim with a little water. Mound the cold filling into the pastry-lined dish, and use the smaller piece of pastry to make the lid in exactly the same way as for single-crust pies. Press the two layers of pastry gently together, then trim away excess, knock up, flute, glaze and make steam slits as described for single-crust pies.

## Tartlet tins

Tartlet tins do not conform to many of the guidelines I have described so far and, being so small, they are a bit awkward for the novice pastry cook to handle. However, they do make very pretty little pies and are well worth trying.

Tartlet tins are sheets of metal, with 6, 9 or 12 indentations, having sloping sides at an angle to the base. Please note that bun tins, which have gently rounded indentations, are unsuitable for double-crust pies. The shape of tartlet tins makes unmoulding somewhat tricky, so, unlike other tins, they need to be lightly greased before lining with shortcrust.

The pastry needs to be rolled out slightly more thinly than usual – not more than 3 mm/⅛ inch thick – and to minimise the handling of the pastry it is best to roll out all the pastry in one piece and to cut out the shapes from it.

Use a cutter the diameter of the top of each hollow to make the lids, and a cutter approximately 2½ cm/1 inch larger to make the linings. Dip the cutting edge in a little flour and stamp the cutter firmly down into the pastry. Lift it up and off cleanly – a twisting movement would distort and tear the pastry. Tap the cutter if necessary to release the circle of pastry. Cut out all the lids first, then the linings. This is because you may need to re-roll the trimmings in order to cut out the last few circles and, since re-rolled pastry never looks so attractive, it is sensible to use these pieces where they will be least noticeable.

Press the linings gently into the tins and mound the filling. The best way to seal these tiny pies is to brush the edges of the pastry lids with a little water, then lay them damp side down over the filling and pinch the pastry edges of lid and lining together to seal. Glaze, make steam holes with the point of a skewer, and chill for 5 minutes before baking.

Always let these tiny cooked pies stand in their tins for at least 2 minutes before unmoulding, so the pastry will shrink away slightly from the sides of the tin: this makes it easier to slip a palette knife round the edge of each pie and to ease it out of the tin.

## Baking shortcrust

The contrast of a hot oven and cool pastry causes the rapid expansion of air trapped in the dough which gives shortcrust its characteristic light texture. For this reason, the oven should always be heated to the correct temperature – usually gas 5–6/190–200°C/375–400°F, – before the pastry is put into it, and the pastry should be chilled for 5 minutes between shaping and baking.

A dry atmosphere is important for crisp results, so do not bake shortcrust while cooking other foods that produce steam in the oven.

When making flans, tarts and double-crust pies it is a good idea to put a baking tray into the oven when you turn it on. The tray will heat up with the oven and, when the flan tin or pie dish is placed on it, provide an extra source of heat to help crisp the base of the pastry as it cooks. I may add that a baking tray has spared me some messy oven-cleaning operations on occasions when I have over-filled pastry cases and fillings have bubbled over during cooking.

Shortcrust only needs 20 minutes or so to cook through. It *can* be cooked for up to an hour without spoiling – and this amount of time is often necessary for pies in order to cook the filling as well as the pastry. Richer pastries, such as puff or flaky, are much more flexible about cooking time, and this is why they are usually preferred for meat pies.

## Blind baking

When a flan or tart is baked with a filling, the weight and volume of the filling help to keep the pastry base flat, and to prevent the sides from caving in during cooking. But it is sometimes preferable to cook a pastry case, partially or completely, without the filling that will eventually be served in it. This is called 'blind baking' and involves using a temporary substitute filling to keep the pastry in shape as it cooks.

Cut a circle of greaseproof paper the same size as the original circle of pastry and place it in the chilled pastry-lined tin, so it fits the corners snugly and the sides of the paper stand well above the sides of the tin. Fill it with enough gravel, dried beans, rice or ceramic beads to come about two thirds of the way up the sides of the tin: this will press the pastry against the tin. Place the flan tin on a hot baking tray on an upper shelf of a pre-heated oven and bake for 10 minutes. Then remove the tin from the oven and carefully lift out the greaseproof paper and weights (they can be saved and re-used time and time again for blind baking). You will see that the pastry has begun to colour and has set just enough to hold its own shape, but it still needs further cooking. The question is for how long?

If you want to serve the flan or tart cold with a filling of cold ingredients (whether raw or separately cooked and cooled), the pastry must be 'completely blind baked', until it is cooked right through. In this case put the pastry-lined tin back onto the hot baking tray and bake for about 12 minutes more.

If the flan is to be served hot with a filling cooked in it, the pastry only needs to set a little more before you add the filling. Another 8 minutes and it will be 'partially blind baked'. However, if the filling is to be liquid when put into the flan (as, for instance, are quiche and sweet custard mixtures), brush the pastry base with a little egg white before you put the pastry back into the oven for its 8 minutes: the egg will set a filmy seal over the pastry surface, a precaution against the filling seeping into the pastry when it is added.

## Freezing and storing

Many people like to freeze completely cooked pies, tarts and flans (recommended storage time depends on the filling used), and to freeze the raw dough in convenient-sized batches (allow 2 hours to thaw 250 g/$\frac{1}{2}$ lb shortcrust at room temperature). I have never found this very satisfactory: shortcrust never seems to regain its original lightness after defrosting.

I find it better to store shortcrust in other ways. Pastry made to the 'rubbed in' stage keeps well in a refrigerator for at least a week if it is put into a thick polythene bag, and tied tightly after squeezing any air pockets out of the bag. Cooked shortcrust can be stored for a few days in the form of a completely blind baked pastry shell – unfilled. Pack it carefully in an airtight tin. If the tin is deep, there is less danger of breaking the pastry when you remove it if you stand the pastry on the lid of the tin and invert the tin base over the top. It is a good idea briefly to reheat pre-cooked pastry shells in the oven before using them to ensure the pastry is crisp.

# Hand-made Mayonnaise

## ELIZABETH DAVID

Those who make their mayonnaise in the electric blender will perhaps think it very quaint that anyone should still use the old method of stirring by hand. In some ways I would agree. The electric blender has, after all, revolutionised our cooking lives during the past three decades, and it is only sensible to take every possible advantage of its labour-saving benefits. I would certainly, for example, use the blender when making a mayonnaise in large quantity. Given time, however, I still take pleasure in settling down to make this extraordinary sauce by the old method which to many people now seems laborious. The following notes, therefore, are concerned mainly with hand-made mayonnaise. They may prove useful to those who already know the theory but still find the practice tricky – and there are, I think, many young people today who prefer hand-made to mechanical methods; there are even people who don't possess or can't be bothered with electric blenders and mixers.

1. The fresher your egg or eggs, the easier and quicker it will be to achieve a mayonnaise of the right consistency. Just what this should be is fully described in note 5 below.

2. If you use an olive oil of good quality with a delicate and true taste of the fruit, mayonnaise needs no seasoning other than lemon juice or a very little wine vinegar. With rare exceptions, as for example when destined for a celeriac salad, mustard is ruination to mayonnaise. Pepper is redundant, and surprisingly so is salt, although that is no doubt a matter of taste. Strong condiments are needed only

for mayonnaise made with totally tasteless oil. Even then they should be used very sparingly indeed. In a mayonnaise all seasonings and flavourings are much intensified. Overdone, they produce a sauce approaching perilously near the bottled stuff.

3. Before starting on a mayonnaise, make certain that eggs and oil are both at room temperature. There is no surer way of curdling the sauce than by using ice-cold ingredients, or an ice-cold with a warm one. So if you store your eggs in the refrigerator, remember to take out however many you need in good time. If you have forgotten this precaution, put your egg or eggs in a bowl of warm water for a few minutes before you start work on the sauce. As for the oil, it would be absurd to refrigerate it, and my advice is don't. Instead, keep it at a moderate and constant temperature.

4. The fewer eggs you can manage with, the better the mayonnaise. Beginners may need the reassurance of using two yolks for a small amount of sauce, but with experience most people discover that one large yolk will serve to thicken up to 300 ml/½ pint of oil and often more. Much depends on the quality of both ingredients. And, again, a fresh egg with a good plump yolk works twice as fast as a stale flat one and goes much further.

5. The solid, jelly-like consistency of a true mayonnaise does, of course, take a little longer to achieve by hand than in the blender. Some people never do achieve it, because – lacking faith perhaps – they give up before the stage of maximum absorption and expansion has been reached, thus producing a pouring sauce rather than the emulsified ointment-like substance that a mayonnaise should be. This was very graphically defined in a recipe I came across recently in Cassell's *Book of the Household*, published in 1889, as being 'quite as thick as a pat of butter on a hot day in August. Indeed it would stand up in a tablespoon, so that you could put three or four tablespoons in one spoon at a time, and hold it up in the air and it would not run over.'

The thickening and expanding process starts only when the egg has absorbed a certain quantity of oil, and at this stage the beginner has to have faith and patience. Quite suddenly you find that the sauce has changed from a thick cream into a smooth, shining ointment. From there you persevere until the ointment is so thick and stiff that it is quite difficult to stir in more oil.

6. Experienced mayonnaise-makers tend to plop oil straight from the bottle, not worrying too much about that drop-by-drop business – except for the first minute or two – but probably the most satisfactory and the simplest method is to use a measuring jug. Any jug with a good pouring spout will do – if it is a bad one you waste a lot of oil – and some kitchen shops probably still stock glass oil pourers imported from Spain. These are very effective, and although they slow up the process rather, do give a feeling of safety to the beginner.

7. Separating the eggs is such a basic kitchen operation that it is surprising to find that people are actually frightened of it. Indeed special gadgets have been invented to help the nervous and the inexperienced. In this respect, the best gadget I know is a good fresh egg. Give it a sharp, decisive tap – in the centre – on the rim of the bowl waiting to receive the white. Passing the egg from one half shell to the other, let the white fall into the bowl, giving it a bit of assistance with the shell. The shell can also be used to scoop out any scrap of yolk which has found its way into the white, but with a really fresh egg this doesn't happen, and it hardly takes more than five seconds to separate the egg. For mayonnaise, by the way, it doesn't matter if a little of the white gets into the bowl with the yolk. It can happen, of course, that a stale egg, on being cracked, falls plop into the bowl and cannot thereafter be separated, so you have to start again with another egg. Or give up the whole enterprise and resort to the blender which obligingly makes mayonnaise from the whole egg. It won't make a very good one though, not with a stale, flat egg.

8. The bowl you use for making mayonnaise should be a fairly solid one, one which does not slide about the table as you stir, and if it is wide in proportion to its depth, so much the better. It will be easier to stir the mixture as it thickens. Professional chefs tend to use a balloon whisk for mayonnaise, so they also need a rather large, deep bowl. Old-fashioned home cooks often used to beat the oil into the egg with a fork. Personally I use a tough little boxwood spoon with a rather long handle. It's a question of finding out what suits you best.

9. I find that adding the oil to the egg drop by drop is necessary only in the very early stages, until yolk and oil are securely amalgamated. After that you can plop it in in quite large spoonfuls. The important thing is to stir very firmly after each addition and to wait until the oil is properly integrated before adding more. The stirring or beating must take in *all* the sauce, from the bottom of the bowl and round the sides as well as the top surface. As the sauce thickens and its volume increases, the oil can be added, if you like, in a steady thin stream. On the whole, though, I find it easier to continue with the system of alternately adding and stirring, a system which creates its own rhythm. Every now and again stir in a little lemon juice. Quite quickly, if all has gone well, the mayonnaise becomes so stiff that it is quite difficult to stir. If you think you have enough, stop now. Taste the mayonnaise, add more lemon juice or a few drops of vinegar if necessary. (Careful about the vinegar though. Nothing is easier than to wreck the entire batch of mayonnaise by the careless addition of vinegar. So measure it out into a teaspoon.) If, however, you still need more, you will find that you can go on incorporating oil for quite a long time after the final stage appears to have been reached, and certainly for long after your arm has started to ache. 300 ml/½ pint of oil per egg yolk seems to me about the right proportion, but you could use much more. The stories you hear about people making a washbasin-size bowl of mayonnaise based on a single egg yolk are not just myths.

Given the rarity, though, and the huge cost of good olive oil, it would be a bit reckless to use more than you need just for the sake of a dare, or because you find the process so mesmerising you can't stop the pouring and stirring.

A very important point remains to be made: one of the major troubles about mayonnaise is that when it's good there is seldom quite enough. So don't stop before you are sure there really *is* enough. But be cautious once you have passed the half-pint-to-one-egg level.

10. If you have a mishap and the sauce does separate, the remedy is to start again with a fresh egg yolk in a clean bowl. Add the curdled sauce a little at a time to the new egg. It will soon thicken and solidify.

11. Once your mayonnaise is soundly and securely integrated, it takes really careless treatment to spoil it.

12. If you need to keep the mayonnaise overnight, possibly the most effective way is to cover the whole surface with, first, a thin film of oil, then with a piece of plastic wrap. Store it in a cool place – say about 15°C/60°F – but not in the refrigerator. (Mayonnaise doesn't like extremes of temperature either way.) The idea of the sealing film of oil is to exclude the air and prevent the formation of a skin which often causes the downfall of the sauce. When the time comes to serve it, simply stir in the oil in the routine way and all should be well. I find this method a very useful one. Another way is to stir a tablespoon of boiling water into the mayonnaise when it is ready. This stabilises it, but does thin it very slightly. To some people this is an advantage, and it does make the sauce go further. So much depends upon what it is to accompany.

13. That last sentence brings me to the olive oil itself. I have deliberately left it to the end of these notes. Olive oil addicts and connoisseurs will have their own views and preferences and experience to draw on. They will also, no doubt, have their own sources of supply. Good and authentic olive oil is now so rare and so expensive that advice to use a heavily fruity, green, first-pressing Tuscan

or Italian Riviera oil, or a slightly more refined and subtle golden oil from Provence for a mayonnaise to go with this or that or the other given dish is about as meaningful as telling people that a Chambolle-Musigny 1967 might be better with the pheasant and chestnuts than a Romanée-Conti 1964. So from my own experience, and for the benefit of the few who are interested enough to search out, and both able and willing to pay for, supplies of good olive oils, I'd say it is by no means essential to use a particularly fruity olive oil for mayonnaise, although I do have to say again that it does depend upon what food the sauce is to go with. For coarse white fish, for example, a fruity oil is an advantage. For salmon trout or a delicate poached chicken I use a milder Provence oil. For salmon, which has its own richness, I'd also use a mild oil, or perhaps equal quantities of a fruity oil and a refined, light and fairly tasteless one of a reliable and uniform quality. To the inexperienced I should add a warning about olive oils blended with other oils, usually corn or sunflower seed oil. Not so long ago, in a friend's house, I made a mayonnaise with this type of oil. I came to the conclusion that the blend must have been in the proportion of a quart of sunflower to an ounce of olive oil. A waste of the olive oil, in fact. It must be remembered that in a mayonnaise the taste of the oil is much intensified. Consequently the flavour of the mayonnaise I made with the blended oil was solely of sunflower seed. No amount of extra seasoning in the form of mustard, lemon juice, salt, pepper, could make it edible.

14. Finally, a method of making mayonnaise using one raw and one hard-boiled egg yolk. This combination makes the basis of the modern sauce *rémoulade*, in other words a thick mayonnaise to which chopped herbs, capers, and sometimes anchovies are added. But there's no reason why the basic sauce shouldn't be regarded just as a mayonnaise which is amazingly good tempered, and one which in my experience it is almost impossible to curdle. It's a bit creamier than an ordinary mayonnaise, but particularly

useful when you have to make the sauce in advance and keep it overnight.

All you need to do is extract the yolk from a not-too-hard-boiled egg, mash it to a paste in a bowl, stir in the raw yolk, and when the two are thoroughly blended start adding the oil. Proceed as usual, adding lemon juice or a few drops of vinegar from time to time as the sauce thickens. You need stop only when you think you have enough sauce, or when your arm aches too much to continue, whichever is the soonest. Cover, as before, with a thin film of oil and then with plastic wrap. Leave in a cool place, but not in the refrigerator.

If you are intending to treat the sauce as a *rémoulade* rather than as straight mayonnaise, add the *rémoulade* part about an hour before serving. In their simplest form the flavourings consist of a teaspoon each of rinsed, carefully drained, and chopped capers, chopped fresh tarragon, and chopped fresh parsely. Optionally, a few chives cut small, a de-salted and chopped anchovy fillet or two, a very little yellow Dijon mustard (an authentic French one, not an imitation). Should you happen to have rocket, that neglected salad and sauce herb, growing in your herb patch, use a chopped leaf or two instead of mustard. The sauce is good with cold chicken and with the breast of lamb dish called *à la sainte Ménéhould*, in other words braised and cooled breast of lamb, boned, cut into strips, breadcrumbed, and grilled on an iron grid over direct heat. An admirably economical dish.

# Clarified Butter

## ELIZABETH DAVID

Clarified butter is of great importance to good cooking. To the success of shallow frying and sautéing of vegetables, fish, escalopes of veal, liver, in fact anything which should be rapidly cooked in a small amount of fat, it makes the whole difference. Although a proportion of oil added to ordinary butter is quite a good way round the problem of burning and sticking involved in this kind of cooking, if you have clarified butter on hand the problem simply does not arise. What happens is that by ridding the butter of impurities, the residue of buttermilk, salt and sediment which blacken and burn as the butter is subjected to heat, you obtain a very pure frying medium which can be heated to a considerably higher temperature than ordinary butter. Its advantages, then, are obvious, and far outweigh the small amount of trouble involved.

All you need, apart from the butter and a reasonably heavy pan, is a double piece of muslin or cheesecloth, a small sieve, and a jar for storage. I find a wide glass jam jar the most satisfactory and cleanest, but almost any non-porous bowl, jar or crock will do.

Put a slab of butter in a frying pan over low heat and let it melt gently. It must not turn colour, but it should be very thoroughly heated, until the whole surface is bubbling, and the sediment rises to the top. At this stage you can see the cleared, clean, limpid butter under the crust of sediment. Leave it to cool for a few minutes. Line a sieve with the dampened muslin or cheesecloth and place the sieve over the storage jar or bowl. Filter the butter slowly through the muslin, without putting any pressure on it. Cover the jar and store it in the refrigerator. The elements which make butter go rancid have been removed, and it will keep a long time, so it is worth making a certain quantity at a time. One of its great uses is for frying croûtons. A couple of tablespoons go a long way.

For the storage of English potted meats and fish pastes, clarified butter provides the traditional seal, airtight, edible, and visually attractive. The best way to make the seal is to stand the jar of clarified butter in a saucepan of water and heat it gently until the butter is partially melted. Pour it warm over the well chilled and smoothed-down paste or potted fish. Leave to set before returning the pot or pots to the refrigerator.

In old French cookery books clarified butter is sometimes called *beurre cuit*, cooked butter.

# Yogurt

## ELIZABETH DAVID

You don't need electrical gadgets and you don't need 'special' cultures to make yogurt. You don't need padded boxes or those incredibly complicated do-it-yourself incubator tea-cosy things that people used to advocate. I'd never have been capable of making one, so I'm thankful that insulated food jars have taken their place. I have those in the house anyway for ice and picnic food, and I have a beautiful old dairy thermometer with its own wooden case. And I have a very large, old and thick aluminium saucepan to boil the milk in. So I've never bought any special equipment, and I'd find it a bore to use an electrical machine for yogurt, as well as a nuisance to have to house it.

The most effective insulated jars are the kind made by Thermos, called 'the super food flask', but Insulex also make very satisfactory ones. Both brands are stocked by department stores and plenty of other shops. Junket thermometers can be bought in kitchen shops, and it's a measure of the present popularity of yogurt that the correct temperature is now marked on them. Brannan's have also brought out a cheap yogurt thermometer.

I'd advise beginners to start with just one or two half-litre/pint-size jars and buy more as needed.

Personally, I use rich, creamy Jersey milk for my yogurt, but many people prefer skim milk. It's a question of whether or not you're on a low-fat diet.

Bring the milk to a bare simmering point, very slowly, stirring from time to time. The object is to reduce the milk somewhat, quite an important part of yogurt-making. Ideally, the milk should reduce to a little under three quarters of the original amount, but the yogurt still works if you don't have the patience or time to watch the milk that long. When you've let it boil up once, take the milk off the heat, stir it, put in the thermometer and leave it until it registers 54°C/130°F or the temperature marked for yogurt on thermometers. Have your jars ready, and some existing yogurt, preferably Loseley or Chambourcy if you're starting from scratch.

Pour the milk into the insulated jars. Quickly – and very thoroughly – stir in a good big tablespoon of the yogurt for each 600 ml/1 pint of milk used. Clap on the lids of the jars. That's it. In about four to six hours the yogurt will be set. (You don't have to put the jars in a warm place, airing cupboard or any such.)

I nearly always make my yogurt in the evening and leave the jars on the kitchen table until the morning, when I transfer them to the fridge. Yogurt doesn't like to be disturbed when it's newly made. I don't know why but it does seem to be so. Anyway it's a pity to break the lovely creamy crust which forms on the top when you use rich milk.

The basic points to remember about yogurt are that it doesn't work if the milk is too hot or too cold. It shouldn't be hotter than 54°C/130°F or cooler than 46°C/115°F. I think if you know about yeast you also soon understand about yogurt. And of course if you make it regularly, you use your own as the starter. Before long you find you're making yogurt very superior to anything you can buy.

I believe there are many people who think you can't make good yogurt with pasteurised milk. This really is not true. Although I will say that one year when, on a number of occasions, I managed to buy Loseley untreated Jersey milk its yogurt-making performance was spectacular. So was its flavour. Loseley don't use it for their yogurt, though. In the first place, they say the public prefers skim-milk yogurt, and in the second, making it on a commercial scale with untreated milk isn't feasible. Stray and unbeneficial bacteria could wreck a whole batch, and many shops wouldn't stock it anyway. But anyone who has access to a supply of untreated milk should try making yogurt with it.

I should add that if I were going to buy new equipment for yogurt-making I'd invest in a catering-size teflon-lined saucepan. And one more point: when it doesn't suit my timetable to wait around while the boiled milk cools to the appropriate temperature I do the boiling in advance. When it comes to making the yogurt it only takes two or three minutes to warm the milk to the right degree.

## Notes

1. Yogurt made from reduced milk sets much firmer than when the milk used has been simply boiled up and left to cool.

2. Many recipes I have seen recently give temperatures too low for good yogurt-making, and also specify as little as a teaspoon of starter yogurt for 600 ml/1 pint of milk. I find that's not nearly enough.

3. When your yogurt begins to turn out rather thin and watery, it is time to start afresh with a new carton of commercial yogurt. I find this necessary only about once every three months. Advice to buy a fresh carton of commercial yogurt every time you make your own is sometimes given by home economists on the grounds that if you use your own yogurt contamination may occur. So long as you keep your yogurt covered and use meticulously clean spoons and flasks when making each batch, in any case, an essential of all dairy work, this advice may safely be ignored.

# Poached Eggs

## ELIZABETH DAVID

Over the years I think that I have received more pleas for advice on the technique of poaching eggs than on any other aspect of cookery, with the possible exception of how to get the *brûlée* part on *crème brûlée*. But that's another story.

In his book, *The Cook's Paradise*, published in 1749, William Verral put the matter in, one might say, an eggshell.

*'Be sure the eggs are fresh; for, from the experience I have had, I am sure it is not in the power of the best cook in the Kingdom to poach stale ones handsome, notwithstanding they may come all whole out of the shell.'*

There you have it. To produce neat, plump, well shaped and comely poached eggs it is essential to start off with fresh eggs. Not *too* fresh though. A really new-laid egg is not a good subject for poaching. The white separates too easily from the yolk. Three-day old eggs are the ideal, although how, unless one keeps hens, one is ever to know the exact age of an egg is not a problem I can solve. But, like many people who live in big towns, I find that it pays to go to some trouble to discover a shop where the supply of eggs is limited, and the turnover rapid, so that one can always be reasonably sure that the eggs are fresh. And when friends arrive from the country with their own fresh eggs I find that the best way to ensure a few days' supply of nicely poached eggs is to cook them immediately and keep them in a bowl of acidulated water in the refrigerator. This is a most successful system. With the help of Parmesan cheese, breadcrumbs, butter and fresh parsley or tarragon, possibly a little cream, or freshly made tomato sauce, or chopped spinach, delicate and appetising little poached egg dishes can be produced for lunch in a few minutes.

Here is the method. Apart from the fresh eggs – for poaching choose small ones whenever possible – a certain knack is needed. It is one which is easily acquired, but until the simple technique has been mastered it is advisable not to attempt to poach more than two or three eggs in one go.

Utensils required are an ordinary saucepan of 1½–2 litre/3-4 pint capacity and with a cover, a long-handled perforated metal spoon, a bowl and a couple of small cups or saucers. I find that a timer is also indispensable.

Three-quarters fill the saucepan with water, bring this to simmering point, add a tablespoon of wine vinegar. Break the eggs into the cups or saucers, slide them into the gently simmering water. Count thirty. Turn off the heat. Quickly, with the edge of your metal spoon, roll each egg over once or twice. This sounds dangerous but – always provided that the eggs are in the right condition – I assure you that it

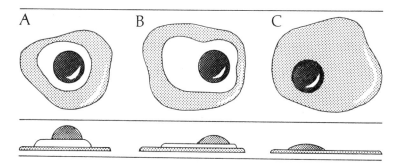

**A.** A fresh egg should have three distinct parts: the yolk, a clear translucent white of gelatinous consistency, and an outer layer of thin white.
**B.** An egg that is less fresh will spread further on the plate, the two layers of white will be mingling and the yolk flattening.
**C.** An egg that is stale will look like this, with a thin runny white which spreads out a long way, and a yolk which is flat and may break easily.

works. If any of the white of the eggs has separated and floated to the surface, skim it off.

Now cover the saucepan and leave the eggs for three minutes.

Have ready a bowl of cold water to which you have added a few drops of wine or tarragon vinegar.

With your perforated spoon lift out the poached eggs and drop them gently into the cold water. This immediately arrests the cooking, so that when you come to reheat the eggs they will still remain tender and soft. Any trimming of the whites which may be necessary can be done at a later stage.

Cover the bowl and store the eggs on the bottom shelf of the refrigerator. If not used within two or three days, renew the slightly vinegared water and return the bowl to the refrigerator.

A week is the maximum time I have stored poached eggs in this manner.

## Notes

1. I find that it is not very practical to make more than one batch of poached eggs without boiling fresh water and vinegar. The water becomes cloudy, and requires much skimming, and often the second or third batch of eggs looks messy. So the sooner one can acquire the knack of poaching several eggs at a time in a large pan, the quicker it will be to poach say half a dozen eggs, so often called for in those recipes which start off by telling you in such a wonderfully carefree way to 'have ready ten nicely poached eggs'.

2. No matter how fresh eggs may be, some are just better than others – plumper, with whites which coagulate more perfectly, so sometimes it is not necessary to turn the eggs over in the water. One sees that the whites have of themselves formed a beautiful, shapely covering for the yolks.

3. Some cooks use a shallow sauté pan rather than a saucepan for the poaching of eggs. I find that it matters little

which is used. Possibly a sauté pan is best for a quantity of eggs, a saucepan for just two or three. Just as for scrambled eggs, omelettes, fried eggs and boiled eggs, the choice of pan is a matter of personal preference. Any law laid down would be arbitrary.

# Preserving

## PRUDENCE LEITH

Preserving is the most satisfyingly scientific of all branches of cookery. Rows of gleaming jam jars on the larder shelf is a romantic image, but achieving the row is a practical business where sugar temperatures and correct proportions are more important than creative inspiration. This is not to say that there is no room for experiment. The imaginative cook could spend a lifetime inventing new preserves and the chances are that most of them would be good and many outstanding. But few of them would be preserves at all (that is, few would *keep*) if the cook did not understand the principles of preserving, and stick to the rules.

Strictly, any food treated so that it will not go bad (i.e. food which is frozen, dried, smoked, bottled etc.) is a preserve. But this chapter deals with those preserves most usually made at home, and not dependent on refrigeration. They are the traditional jams, marmalades, candied and bottled fruits that stretched the summer crops through the winter before the freezer made nonsense of the seasons.

The terms for preserved foods are used, confusingly, to mean different things in different countries, so I should perhaps say what is meant by them here.

**Chutney:** a mixture of fruit and vegetables cooked with sugar and vinegar to a thick, jammy consistency.

**Pickle:** fruit or vegetables preserved in vinegar.

**Jam:** a preserve made from small whole fruits or large

cut-up fruits cooked with sugar. The consistency should be soft enough to spread, but not runny.

**Jelly** is made from strained fruit juices, is clear, and should hold its shape.

**Marmalade** is citrus jam or jelly.

**Fruit cheese** is similar to jam, but made with fruit pureés rather than whole or cut-up fruit. It is cooked to a paste, and contains enough sugar for preservation providing it is kept in a cool place. Sometimes cheeses are boiled down or dried sufficiently to roll into slabs or balls when cold, to be eaten like candy.

**Fruit butter** is similar to fruit cheese, but contains les sugar and is not so thick. It makes good tart fillings.

**Fruit curd** is made from acidic fruit, sugar, butter and eggs.

**Preserve or conserve:** whole fruits, or ginger, in extremely thick syrup. Eaten sliced on buttered bread or in very small quantities with whipped cream as a dessert.

**Bottled goods:** cooked fruit or tomatoes in syrup or water, sterilised in a jar with an airtight lid. The process used is almost identical to that of commercial canning.

**Candied fruit:** whole cooked fruits impregnated with concentrated sugar syrup, then partially dried.

**Glacé fruit:** candied fruits given a sugar glaze after candying.

**Crystallised flowers:** small whole flowers or separate petals coated with egg white, dusted with fine sugar, then dried.

## Equipment

No special equipment is needed for preserving, except preserving jars for bottling, the cook being able to manage perfectly well with ordinary saucepans, ladles, etc. But, for anyone making preserves often or in large quantities, some extras are worth having:

**Preserving pans.** Unlike most saucepans, preserving pans need not be heavy and thick. They are usually comparatively thin-bottomed, which means speedy transference of heat. Most preserves are rapidly boiled and frequently stirred to prevent the burning which might otherwise occur in thin-bottomed pans. Copper and brass preserving pans are pretty, but take a deal of cleaning and should not be used for cooking anything with vinegar in it, or for soaking or macerating acidic fruit, because the acid may react with the metal, spoiling the taste and colour of the preserve and perhaps rendering it mildly poisonous. Aluminium pans are fine for fast cooking, even of high-acid preserves, but acid foods should not be left in them for long periods. Enamelled or stainless steel pans can safely be left in contact with food. A pressure-cooker or large saucepan will do well as a preserving pan, provided it is not filled more than one-third full. The sloping sides and good width of a true preserving pan limit the splashing of hot syrup, rather as waves will splash less against a sloping beach than against a vertical cliff face.

A **sugar thermometer**, preferably calibrated in both centigrade and fahrenheit, is useful for jam-making, candying and bottling.

A **set of accurate scales** takes a lot of the guesswork out of jam-making.

A **perforated skimmer** speeds up the skimming of jam, and is useful for fishing out fruit stones. Also, in the absence of jar lifters, a skimmer can be slid under the jars to lift them clear of the water, enabling the cook to grasp the jar top with an oven glove.

A **pair of jar lifters** (tong-like instruments) is useful for lifting bottled fruit out of sterilising water.

A **jam funnel** permits the filling of jam jars without mess. A large metal ladle with a pouring lip or a metal or heatproof glass jug will do.

## Specialist equipment

**Jam covers.** Paper cover are bought in packets from stationers or chemists. Well-fitting metal screw tops (but not plastic ones) or a covering of melted paraffin wax will do. See p. 69–70 for instructions

**Preserving jars.** These are essential for bottling. They are described in detail on p. 85.

Jars are re-usable indefinitely, but the rubber rings, or rubberised lids, must be renewed for eachbottling. Jars with chipped rims will not give a proper seal, and rusty or bent metal parts should be replaced.

**Pickle jars and stoppers.** Nice-looking wide-necked glass and stoneware jars with cork or glass stoppers can be bought for storing pickles, but any wide-necked non-plastic jar is adequate. To cover, use a few layers of waxed paper secured with a rubber band.

### THE JAM FAMILY

The preservation of jams, jellies, and marmalades depends on five factors:

1. **The presence of pectin.** Pectose, a gum-like substance present to a greater or lesser degree in all fruit (it sometimes emerges in glassy globules near the stem of ripe plums), converts, under heat, to pectin. Providing the proportions of acid and sugar in the jam are correct, and the correct temperature is reached, pectin will give the jam a jelly-like set when cold. Unset jam is more likely to ferment than well set jam.

Perfectly ripe, or *slightly* underripe fruit, is higher in pectin than overripe fruit. Certain fruits contain more pectin than others – notably, apples, quinces, damsons, plums, lemons, redcurrants and gooseberries. Low-pectin fruits such as strawberries, rhubarb, mulberries and pears need the addition of commercial pectin or lemon juice to obtain a set. The addition of a small quantity of high-pectin fruit or juice will also do the trick.

**Testing for pectin.** A simple test will ascertain whether or not the fruit to be made into jam has enough pectin: once the prepared fruit is simmered, but before the sugar is added, put a teaspoon of the fruit liquid into a glass. Allow to cool, then add 3 teaspoons methylated spirit. After a minute or so the mixture will have clotted into a jelly. If the jelly is in a single, largish clot, and fairly firm, the pectin content is high. If the clots are small, soft and numerous, or the mixture has not formed lumps at all, additional pectin will be necessary.

2. **The presence of sufficient acid.** Acid prevents the growth of bacteria, and it prevents the crystallisation of sugar during storage, but its main function is to act with the sugar and pectin to form a set. Additional acid may be added in the form of citric acid, tartaric acid, or acidic fruit juice such as lemon or redcurrant.

3. **The presence of sugar.** A high concentration of sugar is necessary to act with the acid and pectin to obtain a set. In addition, the sugar itself is a preservative.

4. **Sterilisation.** Micro-organisms, which, if left to multiply in the jam, would cause spoilage, are eliminated by boiling. Jam jars, lids and jugs used in the potting process should, ideally, also be sterilised. There are several methods of sterilising equipment: jars and lids etc. may be heated in a deep saucepan of water and boiled for 20 minutes, or they may be sterilised with patent sterilising solutions marketed for the treatment of babies' bottles etc. But the easiest

method is simply to wash the jars, lids (with cardboard inserts removed), ladle, jug and other equipment in a weak household bleach solution, and then to pour a kettle of boiling water over them to wash away any taste of chlorine. Wipe them well with a freshly laundered tea towel, or dry in a coolish oven. Do not let your fingers touch the inside of the jam jars. The only implements that need not be treated are the wooden spoons, skimmers and preserving pan – prolonged contact with the boiling jam will sterilise them.

5. **Sealing.** The exclusion of any new micro-organisms is as important as the elimination of the existing ones described above. The most effective seal is an ordinary metal screw top such as those used by commercial jam-makers. The only old tops not suitable are plastic ones, which do not give a good seal, or rusty metal ones. The metal lid need not be enamelled or coated with plasticised paint if care is taken to prevent the jam touching the lid. If the jar is to sit on the larder shelf for a year, unlined metal lids with the old cardboard inserts removed are safe enough, but if the jam is to be posted to a friend or sold at the church bazaar the inside of the lid should be the enamelled type, or a piece of plastic film could be put over the jar before screwing down the lid. This will ensure that the acid in the jam cannot come into contact with – and subsequently corrode – the metal.

The jam surface must be at least 1 cm/$\frac{1}{2}$ inch below the lid, which is screwed tight while the jam is still boiling hot. The trapped air contracts as it cools, forming a partial vacuum which locks the lid on tight.

The more usual, though more bothersome, way of sealing jam jars is to cover them with paper jam covers: as soon as the jam is potted, lay a waxed paper disc directly on the hot jam surface, waxed side down. The disc should fit the exposed jam surface exactly (the covers are available to fit different-sized jars) without crumpling. Next, carefully wet one side only of the cellophane cover, and lay it, wet side up, over the jar top. Secure with the rubber band, then carefully stretch the cellophane by pulling gently at the edges. The wet paper will stretch slightly, then as it dries and the pot cools, the paper will shrink round the jar top, forming an airtight seal.

The third, and probably most sure, way of sealing jam jars is to cover the jam surface with liquid paraffin wax. For this the jam must be filled to the brim of the jars, or very nearly. The jam is then left to cool and set. A thin layer of melted wax is then poured over the surface of the jam, and left to cool and harden. Any spaces or holes found round the edge of the wax once it has solidified can be filled with a further application of wax painted on with a brush. The jam level must be well over the shoulders of the jar, because once the wax is set it cannot be extracted without frustration and mess if it is below the neck. The paraffin in the wax prevents any growth of micro-organisms which might have alighted on the jam as it cooled. Melted white candles make a good substitute for paraffin wax. Put the candles in a glass jar, and melt in a cool oven. Do not leave the brush in the jar after use or it will be stuck fast once the remaining wax is cold.

**The fruit.** Choose just-ripe fruit. Ideally it should be dry (do not pick raspberries or strawberries immediately after rain), and in perfect condition.

**The sugar.** Use granulated, preserving, or lump sugar. All white sugars are equally refined today, giving a clear preserve which needs little skimming. The only advantage of preserving sugar is that the large crystals allow the boiling liquid to circulate round the grains freely. Even caster may be used, but it needs constant stirring as it settles like a sandbank on the bottom of the pan. Do not use brown sugar, which spoils the colour of the jam and gives it a pronounced caramel taste.

## Stages in jam-making

1. Wash (or preferably sterilise) jam jars, lids and ladle, jug or jam funnel. Dry them in the oven or with a newly laundered cloth. To calculate the number of jars needed, reckon on the finished yield being double the weight of the sugar needed. It may be less, but it is better to have too many jars ready than to be left with hot jam and no jars to pot it in.

2. Put the jars into a low oven to keep warm.

3. Prepare the fruit, stoning if necessary. Do not wash unless dusty.

4. Put the fruit in the pan, just cover with water and set to simmer until soft.

5. Test for pectin if unsure of the setting ability of the fruit (see p. 68). Add the juice of one large lemon for every 500 g/1 lb of fruit if the pectin content is low. Or omit the test and add the lemon juice anyway, on the better-safe-than-sorry principle.

6. Warm the sugar in a low oven. When it is added to the fruit it will then not lower the temperature too much, and cause prolonged cooking which could impair the colour of the jam.

7. Bring the fruit to a good boil. Tip in the sugar and stir, without reboiling, until the sugar has dissolved.

8. Once the sugar has dissolved boil rapidly, stirring gently but frequently. If whole fruit jam is wanted but the fruit is likely to break up (e.g. strawberries) boil gently.

9. When the mixture begins to look and smell like jam (anything from 5 to 30 minutes) test for setting. It is important not to overboil since this can make the colour too dark and the texture too solid. It will also ruin the flavour. If using a thermometer, setting point is 105° C/220° F.

**To test for setting,** put a teaspoon of the jam on to an ice-cold saucer and return it to the ice compartment or freezer to cool rapidly. When cold, push it gently with a finger. If setting point is reached the jam will have a slight skin, which will wrinkle. If a finger is drawn through the jam, it should remain separated, not run together. Also, if the wooden spoon is held high over the pan, the last drops will run from it reluctantly, quivering on the brink, rather than in a quick stream.

10. As soon as the setting proves positive, draw the jam off the heat. Carefully skim off any scum. (It is a mistake to skim jam while boiling – too much clear jam is lost.)

11. If the jam contains whole fruit, or large pieces of fruit, allow it to cool for 15 minutes or so. This will slightly thicken the syrup which, when potted, will hold the fruit in suspension. It will rise to the top of the jar if the syrup is too hot and runny.

12. Put the hot jars close together on a board or tray and fill them with the aid of jug, ladle or funnel.

13. Seal at once (see p. 69).

14. Wipe any stickiness off the jar sides with a hot, damp, clean cloth.

15. Leave undisturbed overnight.

16. Label the jars with date and jam type.

17. Remove to a cool, airy, dark place. Because the home sealing of jams is not totally reliable, every effort needs to be made to discourage moulds. Warm, steamy, unventilated places encourage them. Prolonged bright light will affect the clear bright colour of jam, but this is a secondary requirement. Refrigerating jams is not recommended – moulds and bacteria are discouraged, but the low temperature usually causes the sugar in the jam to crystallise.

## Marmalades

The brief simmering given to most fruit would not be sufficient to soften the tough skins of citrus fruits which are included in marmalades. For this reason the skins are chopped, minced or sliced, soaked overnight to soften them, then simmered in plenty of water (at least five times the volume of prepared fruit) for two or more hours until glassy-looking and soft. The pips (tied loosely in a muslin bag) are soaked and cooked with the skins as they contain valuable pectin. When the skins are soft, the pip bag is squeezed to extract liquid and pectin, then discarded. The juice is added with the sugar, and the marmalade is boiled to a set like jam.

*Clear marmalade* is made by straining the liquid into a clean pan before adding the juice and sugar. Of course the pips need not be bagged as they will be strained out with the other solid ingredients. '*Golden Shred*' type marmalade is made by cooking the finely pared rind, cut into needle-shreds, in a muslin bag in the liquid. After the pips, pith etc. have been strained out, the shreds are tipped into the liquid with the juice and sugar.

## Jellies

Jellies are the easiest preserves to make, though the yield is considerably less per pound of fruit than that of jams.

## Stages in jelly-making

1. Cut the fruit up roughly if it is large. Do not skin, pip, de-stalk or core – even the odd apple twig or blackcurrant leaf will do no harm.

2. Put the fruit into the preserving pan, adding enough water so that the fruit just floats. Simmer until the fruit is soft. Mash roughly.

3. Fix a jelly-bag or several thicknesses of muslin (or a piece of flannel, or any tightly woven, colour-fast cloth) over a clean bucket. There is no need to sterilise equipment as the juice will be reboiled later.

4. Tip the liquid and fruit into the cloth and allow it to drip, at its own pace, through the cloth into the bucket. Do not stir, squeeze or try to hurry the process. Forcing the pace produces murky jelly.

5. Next day (or several hours later when all the juice is through) measure the liquid. For every 600 ml/1 pint of juice measure 500 g/1 lb sugar.

6. Test the juice for pectin if unsure of setting ability (see p. 68).

7. Sterilise the glass jars etc. (p. 68). Jars from spices or herbs or bottled cream are best because they are small enough to be consumed at a sitting and look good on the table if to be served with roast lamb or turkey.

8. Return the juice to the clean preserving pan, add the sugar and boil until setting point is reached (105° C/220° F).

9. Pour at once into clean, hot, dry jars.

10. Seal as for jam. The paraffin wax method is perhaps the best for small jars or tumblers, most of which do not have screw tops and are too small for standard paper covers.

## Problems

The three main dangers of jam-making are *fermentation, crystallisation* and the appearance of *mould*.

**Mould** is caused by using unsterilised jars, covering the jam when lukewarm, imperfect sealing, or a damp or too warm storage place. The mould is harmless, and should be scraped off the jam with a spoon, and the jam consumed quickly, before new mould appears.

Many cooks make mould-free jam without bothering to sterilise equipment or being overly careful about sealing. But once mould does appear in a storeroom cupboard or larder it is extremely difficult to eradicate. Year after year any badly sealed or imperfectly made jam inevitably acquires a film of mould. The only real answer is to make sure everything in the storeroom is airtight (removing any food which is not, which must then not go back) and to wash walls, floor and ceiling (and all containers) with a strong bleach or anti-fungicidal solution.

**Fermentation** (when the jam goes fizzy and bad) is similarly caused by using wet or dirty jars, or by too warm storage, but the commonest cause is non-setting of the jam. If the jam is too runny because of insufficient boiling, or because there is too little pectin, acid, or sugar, fermentation is more than likely. Fermented jam cannot be rescued.

**Crystallisation** of the sugar in the jam is usually caused by too cold storage, but may also be the result of insufficient acid (or conversely too much sugar), boiling the syrup before the sugar is dissolved, or leaving the jam uncovered.

## A FEW JAMS, JELLIES AND MARMALADES

## *Apple and blackberry jam*

| 500 g | 1 lb | peeled and cored cooking apples |
|-------|------|--------------------------------|
| 500 g | 1 lb | blackberries |
| 1 kg | 2 lb | sugar |
| 75 ml | 2½ fl oz | water |

Follow the instructions on p. 71, but add the blackberries once the apples have cooked until tender in the water. Simmer 10 minutes then add sugar and boil fast to set.

## *Damson jam*

| 1 kg | 2 lb | damsons |
|------|------|---------|
| 1½ kg | 3 lb | sugar |
| 600 ml | 1 pint | water |

Slit each damson from stalk to tip with a knife, cutting through to the stone. As the fruit cooks the stones will float to the surface of the jam and can be skimmed off – less tedious than stoning when raw. Otherwise follow the instructions on p. 71.

## Spiced cranberry jam

| 500 g | 1 lb | cranberries |
|---|---|---|
| 1 kg | 2 lb | sugar |
| 150 ml | ¼ pint | water |
| 1 tsp cinnamon | | |

Follow the instructions on p. 71, adding cinnamon before potting.

## Strawberry jam

| 1 kg | 2 lb | strawberries |
|---|---|---|
| 750 g | 1½ lb | sugar |
| juice of 2 lemons | | |
| 75 ml | 2½ fl oz | water |

Put the water, lemon juice and sugar into the pan and heat slowly, stirring to a syrup. When dissolved, add berries and simmer carefully, stirring gently to set.

## Oxford marmalade

| 1 kg | 2 lb | Seville oranges |
|---|---|---|
| 2 large lemons | | |
| 3 litres | 5 pints | water |
| 2 kg | 4 lb | sugar |
| 2 tbs black treacle | | |

Follow marmalade instructions, p. 72, adding black treacle before potting.

## Clear grapefruit marmalade

| 2 large grapefruit | | |
|---|---|---|
| 4 lemons | | |
| 2½ litres | 4 pints | water |
| 1½ kg | 3 lb | sugar |

Follow clear marmalade instructions, p. 73.

# Mint jelly

| |
|---|
| *apples or quinces* |
| *chopped fresh mint* |
| *sugar* |

Follow jelly instructions, p. 73, adding a cupful of chopped mint for every 600 ml/1 pint of juice before potting.

# Redcurrant and orange jelly

| |
|---|
| *redcurrants* |
| *orange juice* |
| *sugar* |

Follow jelly instructions, p. 73, adding orange juice to roughly equal quantity of stewed redcurrants before straining.

# Fruit cheese

Allow 500 g/1 lb sugar for each 500 g/1 lb prepared fruit. Cook the fruit in a little water until soft. Liquidise and/or push through a sieve. Return to the pan with the sugar. Stir over low heat until the sugar is dissolved, then increase the heat and stir until so thick that a wooden spoon drawn through the mixture will leave 'walls' of fruit purée on each side. Pot in hot, dry, clean jars. Suitable for apricots, damsons, plums, greengages, apples, quinces and other fleshy fruit. Not suitable for oranges, grapes, pineapple or fruit producing clear juice rather than purée.

# Fruit butter

Purée the fruit, then allow 500 g/1 lb sugar (or slightly less) to 600 ml/1 pint purée. Cook until thick. Pot in hot, dry, clean jars, and keep cool. Fruits suitable for cheeses will make good butters too.

## Fruit curds

Put the fruit purée (or juice), butter, sugar and well beaten eggs together in a saucepan, beat until smooth, then cook over moderate heat, stirring until thick. A double saucepan is often recommended but is not strictly necessary. The acid in the fruit prevents the eggs from scrambling into lumps. Pot in hot, clean, dry jars. Keep cool. Eat within a month. (Curds may be thickened to commercial-style consistency by adding a teaspoon or two of slaked cornflour to the simmering mixture.)

Cheeses, butters and curds will keep in a cool larder, but not as reliably as a well set jam. Cooks without old-fashioned larders should perhaps refrigerate them and run the risk of slight crystallisation rather than the risk of fermentation.

## Gooseberry curd

| 1 kg | 2 lb | gooseberries, cooked and sieved |
|------|------|----------------------------------|
| 750 g | 1½ lb | sugar |
| 180 g | 6 oz | butter |
| 4 eggs | | |

## Lemon curd

| juice and finely grated rind of 2 large lemons | | |
|------|------|------|
| 90 g | 3 oz | butter |
| 240 g | 8 oz | sugar |
| 3 eggs | | |

## Orange curd

| juice and finely grated rind of 2 oranges and 2 lemons | | |
|------|------|------|
| 360 g | 12 oz | sugar |
| 120 g | 4 oz | butter |
| 4 eggs | | |

## PICKLES

Pickles (like chutneys, p. 81) are marvellously easy to make. This is because they depend on strong vinegar for their preservation, and so sterilisation of equipment, careful temperature control, elaborate sealing and testing for a set are all unnecessary. The vinegar must contain at least 5% acetic acid to be effective. Malt vinegar is commonly used, but any bought vinegar will do.

Vegetables make the best pickles and may be pickled cooked or raw. Raw vegetables, after such preparation as peeling or slicing, must be salted. This is to draw the juices out of the vegetable before immersing it in vinegar. If the vegetable juices were to leak slowly into the vinegar during storage they would dilute it, so impairing its keeping qualities.

If the vegetables are hard, such as shallots, onions or carrots, they should be soaked overnight in a strong brine, made by dissolving common salt in eight times its volume of water. Heating the brine will hasten the dissolving, but it should be cooled again before immersing the vegetables. Prick hard vegetables deeply all over with a stainless steel needle to facilitate the penetration of the salt and the leakage of the vegetable juices. Hold them under the brine with a wooden board or a heavy plate. 'Wet' vegetables such as cucumber or marrow can simply be sprinkled heavily with salt and left to disgorge their juices. After brining, rinse well, then dry in a cloth, pack into storage jars and pour over cold pickling vinegar. Cover the top to prevent evaporation and leave to mature and mellow for six months or more. Remember that even the fumes of vinegar will corrode metal lids.

If a mild-tasting pickle with diluted vinegar is wanted, the vegetable must be cooked and bottled as described for beetroot on p. 81, using about 2 parts vinegar to 3 parts water.

**Pickling vinegar** can be bought commercially, but is easily made and the spices can be varied according to taste. This is a good all-purpose recipe:

| |
|---|
| 1¼ litres /2 pints vinegar |
| 1 tbs mace blades |
| 2 cinnamon sticks |
| 2 tsp allspice berries |
| 2 tsp black peppercorns |
| 2 tsp mustard seed |
| 4 whole cloves |
| 1 chilli pepper, split in half |
| 1 thumb-sized piece root ginger, split or sliced |

Bring everything to the boil slowly, remove from the heat, and leave to cool. Remove the spices if liked, or put them into the jars with the pickles.

### A FEW PICKLES

## *Dill cucumber*

Prick whole small cucumbers and leave overnight, heavily dredged with salt. Rinse very well. Squeeze dry and cover with pickling vinegar containing (per 600 ml/1 pint) 2 tsp mustard seed, 2 garlic cloves, 180 g/6 oz sugar and a good handful fresh dill weed or 1 tbs dill seeds.

## *Pickled onions*

Prick peeled onions deeply with stainless steel needle. Soak 48 hours in brine. Rinse. Squeeze well. Cover with pickling vinegar.

# Pickled eggs

Boil eggs for 12 minutes and shell while warm. Pack into jars and cover with pickling vinegar made with white malt or wine vinegar (which does not discolour the eggs).

# Pickled beetroot

Cook beetroots until tender in salted water. Peel and slice or leave whole if small. Pack in jars. Cover with pickling vinegar. (For a milder beetroot use 75% water and 25% vinegar.) Pack into preserving jars. Process briefly to sterilise (p. 86).

## CHUTNEYS

Chutneys, jam-like mixtures with a definite vinegar tartness, are usually made with fruit or with soft vegetables such as courgettes, marrows or tomatoes, flavoured with onion and spices.

The salt and sugar in chutneys are not important for their preservative powers. The boiling of the mixture destroys any micro-organisms present, and the large proportion of vinegar (malt or any other) prevents the growth of new ones. Sealing should be tight enough to prevent evaporation, but need not be hermetic. See the remarks about sealing pickles, which apply equally to chutneys.

Chutneys improve with keeping, as they lose their initial harshness. They are best eaten between six months and two years after making.

One of the satisfactory aspects of chutney-making is that overripe, bruised or damaged vegetables or fruit, unsuitable for almost anything else, can be used, with the imperfect parts removed. Fruit and vegetables should be cut up small enough to form a soft amalgam – whole apricots or large pieces of mango look nice in chutneys, but once they are eaten, the remaining chutney is unappetisingly mean.

## Stages in chutney-making

1. Prepare the ingredients: soak large dried fruits (like prunes or dried apricots) until tender. If using whole citrus fruit slice finely and simmer in water until soft, then drain. Otherwise just wash, peel, and cut up fruit and vegetables as appropriate.

2. Put everything into a saucepan or preserving pan (not a copper, brass or unlined iron one) and simmer very gently until the toughest ingredients are softened.

3. Boil rapidly until thick and syrupy. Stir constantly towards the end of cooking to prevent burning.

4. Pot in hot, dry, clean jars. Cover.

### A FEW CHUTNEYS

(Weights given are before peeling, coring, soaking etc.)

## Green tomato and apple chutney

| 1½ kg | 3 lb | green tomatoes |
|---|---|---|
| 1 kg | 2 lb | apples (any kind) |
| 2 large onions, chopped | | |
| 120 g | 4 oz | sultanas |
| 1 tsp salt | | |
| 1 tsp ground ginger | | |
| ½ tsp ground nutmeg | | |
| ½ tsp white pepper | | |
| a pinch of ground allspice | | |
| 600 ml | 1 pint | vinegar |
| 360 g | 12 oz | granulated or preserving sugar |

## Prune and hazelnut chutney

| 500 g | 1 lb | stoned prunes, soaked |
|---|---|---|
| 500 g | 1 lb | cooking apples |

| 300 g | 10 oz | dark brown sugar |
|---|---|---|
| 300 ml | ½ pint | wine vinegar |
| 120 g | 4 oz | hazelnuts |
| ½ tsp tumeric | | |
| 1 tsp ground cinnamon | | |
| 1 tsp ground allspice | | |
| a pinch of ground cayenne | | |

## Marrow and blackberry chutney

| 1 kg | 2 lb | marrow |
|---|---|---|
| 500 g | 1 lb | blackberries |
| 750 g | 1½ lb | apples (any kind) |
| 1 large onion | | |
| 250 g | 8 oz | sultanas |
| 250 g | 8 oz | sugar |
| 300 ml | ½ pint | vinegar |
| 1 tsp ground ginger | | |
| 2 tsp mixed spice | | |
| 1 tsp mustard seed | | |

## Mango chutney

| 500 g | 1 lb | mangoes |
|---|---|---|
| 500 g | 1 lb | cooking apples |
| 1 medium onion | | |
| 360 g | 12 oz | brown sugar |
| 1 tsp ground ginger | | |
| 1 tsp salt | | |
| 600 ml | 1 pint | vinegar |

## Piccalilli

This is a cross between a pickle and a chutney, the ingredients being first soaked in brine, then covered with a hot cooked sauce. It can be made with any mixed vegetables, but usually contains at least 20% tiny cauliflower florets.

| | | |
|---|---|---|
| 1 kg/1 lb (prepared weight) mixed vegetables, e.g. cauliflower, green peppers, cabbage, green beans, marrow, shallots, onions, cucumber | | |
| brine made of 600 ml/1 pint water and 60 g/2 oz common salt | | |
| 1 heaped tsp cornflour for a thickish sauce | | |
| 1 tbs dry English mustard | | |
| 15 g | ½ oz | turmeric powder |
| 600 ml | 1 pint | vinegar |
| 120 g | 4 oz | sugar |

Put the finely sliced or chopped vegetables in the brine and leave to soak overnight. Drain and dry well, then pack into scrupulously clean jars.

In the bottom of a saucepan mix the cornflour, mustard and turmeric with a tablespoon or so of the vinegar until smooth. Add the rest of the vinegar and the sugar and, stirring, slowly bring to the boil. Simmer 5 minutes. Pour over the vegetables to cover them, and seal the jars.


## BOTTLING

Our more happy-go-lucky forbears bottled or canned everything – meat, fish, vegetables and fruit. But I would only recommend fruit-bottling. Because fruit is, for the most part, high in acid (and when it is not, lemon juice can be added without spoiling the taste), dangerous bacteria will not be present, and we need only be concerned with brief processing to kill off less harmful moulds and yeasts. Adding acid to vegetables (except beetroot) and to meat ruins the flavour, and the prolonged high temperatures necessary for the safe processing of non-acidic ingredients spoil the texture – hence the pulpy texture of canned carrots and stew. Most fruit contains plenty of fruit acid. The only common fruits low in acid are figs, sweet pears and very ripe tomatoes, and a dash of lemon juice positively improves their taste.

The principles of bottling are simple: the patent seal of

special jars gives a reliably airtight seal, preserving the sterilised food inside. The fruit is always cooked, both to soften it and to sterilise it. This is usually done in syrup, but sometimes in water or brine. The cooking process may take place in the preserving jar, or before the fruit and liquid is transferred to the jar. If the cooking is done in the jars, no further sterilisation is necessary. If it is done before packing into the jars, the filled jars must then be briefly processed by boiling under water or in a pressure-cooker to sterilise them, or the empty jars must be ready-sterilised when the fruit goes into them. This last, however, is not entirely satisfactory – there is always the chance that mould spores will settle during the brief interval between sterilisation and sealing, and live to multiply in the jar. Some cookery books recommend the 'oven method' where jars are heated in the oven, then sealed while hot, but the method is often messy, sometimes dangerous (the jars occasionally crack) and unreliable.

**The preserving jars.** Pre-1980 *Kilner jars* have metal lids with rubber washers incorporated in them. The lids are kept in place by metal screw-bands. Lids must not be re-used as they will not give a good seal twice, and the rubber is perishable. The latest version of the Kilner jar has a glass lid with a loose rubber ring and a polypropylene screw-band. The lid and screw-band are re-usable but the rubber must be renewed for each bottling. Kilner jars are closed loosely before processing, and only tightened fully when they come *out* of the steriliser or saucepan, while still hot. As the hot air inside cools it will contract, pulling the lid on tightly as it does so. The pressure of the partial vacuum will cause metal lids (which start off convex in shape) to 'pop' into a concave position. The sound of this can be alarming but it simply means that a vacuum seal has been achieved.

*Le Parfait jars* have glass lids with loose rubber washers, with the lid held in place by a metal clip. The lid is snapped shut *before* processing. There is sufficient spring in the clip to allow the escape of steam during heating. The lid tightens automatically as the jar cools after processing. Jars are re-usable indefinitely, but the rubber rings, or rubberised metal lids, must be renewed for each bottling. Jars with chipped rims will not give a proper seal, and rusty or bent metal parts should be replaced.

**Raw pack or cooked pack?** Delicate fruit, such as berries or tomatoes, are generally put into the jars raw, covered with boiling liquid and processed (sterilised) as briefly as possible. This is called the *raw pack method*.

Fruit that takes an uncertain time to soften (such as firm pears which, depending on variety, can take anything from 10 to 45 minutes) are best cooked in syrup in the conventional open pan, and processed in the jars afterwards. This is the *cooked pack method*.

Ripe pears, peaches, plums, apples and other fairly predictable fruits can be done by either method.

**Processing the jars.** There are two methods of processing. The first is simply to immerse the jars in a deep saucepan of boiling water and to boil steadily for the recommended time. This is the *boiling water-bath method*. The second is to put them into a pressure-cooker containing very little water and to process them for a much shorter time, under pressure. This is the *pressure method*.

## Bottling by the raw pack method

1. Make sure that rubber seals or metal lids have not been used before and that jars are clean.

2. Fill the jars with the raw fruit, shaking them down to pack well, but without bruising.

3. Top up with boiling syrup (or water as appropriate), leaving the neck of the jar clear.

4. If using Kilner jars, put on the lids and screw-bands and close only loosely. If using Le Parfait jars, put new

rubbers in place round the lids and clamp down with the wire clip.

5. Process for the recommended time (see table, p. 90).

6. Remove the jars from the water and, if using Kilner jars, tighten the lids immediately.

7. Leave undisturbed until cold.

8. Test the seal – unscrew the Kilner bands or unclip the Le Parfait clamps, and lift the jars, one by one, by their now apparently unsecured lids. The vacuum seal should be tight enough to allow lifting the jars without breaking the seal. If the lid comes off, the jar must be re-processed with a new lid or washer, or the fruit should be refrigerated and eaten within a few days, which is usually easier.

## Bottling by the cooked pack method

1. Stew the fruit in syrup in the usual way.

2. Check that jars are clean, and metal lids or washers new.

3. Pack the hot fruit into the jars, and cover with the cooking syrup, filling the jars to the base of the neck, leaving a good 1 cm/$\frac{1}{2}$ inch headroom.

4. Clamp down Le Parfait lids. Close Kilner lids loosely.

5. Process very briefly (to sterilise the contents without further cooking). Follow the timings on the table, p. 90.

6. Lift the jars from the water, and screw Kilner jar lids on tightly.

7. Leave undisturbed until cold, then test for sealing as in raw pack method.

## Processing by the boiling water-bath method

1. Put a cloth in the bottom of a saucepan which must be taller than the jars to be processed. Stand as many filled jars in as can be fitted. If they look as though they will rattle and possibly crack against each other, put more cloths between them.

2. Cover the jars with boiling water to submerge them.

3. Boil for the required time, topping up the water if it goes below the jar tops. (*Note*. In the absence of a sufficiently deep saucepan or preserving pan, it is possible to improvise a lid with a folded cloth covered with foil, to contain the steam which will then sterilise the bottle tops. But the covering must go right over the jars and be tucked or tied round the saucepan to minimise escape of heat, the water level must at least reach the bottle necks and the processing time should be increased by 20%.)

## Processing by the pressure method

High-domed pressure-cookers are best as they take tall jars.

1. Put $2\frac{1}{2}$ cm/ 1 inch of water in the bottom of the cooker and put in the trivet or a folded cloth.

2. Put in the closed jars and prevent the possibility of cracking by putting cloths between the jars if they are not tightly wedged.

3. Put the lid on the cooker. Bring it to $2\frac{1}{2}$ kg/5 lb or $3\frac{1}{2}$ kg/7 lb pressure, depending on the cooker (Tefal cookers are all pre-set at $3\frac{1}{2}$ kg/7 lb).

4. Time the processing from the second the cooker reaches pressure. Accuracy is all.

5. Allow the pressure to reduce slowly. Do not be tempted to release the pressure rapidly or the suction effect may draw the cooked syrup up through the jar lids, causing mess and possibly spoiling the chances of a good seal.

6. Once pressure is reduced, but while the cooker is still very hot, remove the lid and lift out the hot jars. If the cooker lid is impossible to remove, it has been over-cooled. Just reheat briefly.

## Syrups for fruit-bottling

To make a heavy syrup suitable for peaches or sour plums,

bring equal quantities (measured by volume) of sugar and water to the boil together. For a medium syrup use 2 parts water to 1 of sugar, and for a light syrup use 3 parts water to 1 of sugar. Add about a tablespoon of lemon juice for every 600 ml/1 pint of syrup if bottling ripe pears or figs.

## CANDIED FRUITS, GLACÉ FRUITS AND CRYSTALLISING

Confusingly, the words 'candied', 'glacé' and 'crystallised' are used by manufacturers and public to mean any one of the confections described below. In all of them the only preservative used is sugar.

**Candied fruits** are given repeated soakings in hot syrup to saturate and impregnate them with sugar. The length of time the process takes – anything up to 14 days – will depend on the size, dryness, ripeness and type of fruit, and on the concentration of the sugar syrup used. It is not possible to calculate exactly when fruit will be ready, but it is easy to tell once it is: the fruit will feel firm when cold, and will have a glassy transparency.

**Glacé fruits** are first candied, then given a final coating of sugar glaze which dries to a slightly flaky, crusty skin.

**Crystallised fruits** are first candied, then given a grainy finish.

**Crystallised flowers** are coated with egg white and sugar, and then dried.

## *Stages in candying*

1. Choose perfect, not overripe, fruit. Pears, redcurrants, pineapple, whole kumquats, figs, cherries, slices of orange or lemon, may be candied, as can chestnuts or pieces of angelica stem. De-stalk, peel, slice etc. as appropriate.

## Bottling instructions

| Fruit | Method | Syrup | Time in boiling water bath | Time in pressure-cooker |
|---|---|---|---|---|
| Whole peeled dessert apples | Cooked pack | Thin | 1 kg/2 lb jars: 10 minutes<br>2 kg/4 lb jars: 15 minutes | 1 kg/2 lb jars: 1 minute<br>2 kg/4 lb jars: 2 minutes |
| Sliced cooking apples | Raw pack | Thin | 1 kg/2 lb jars: 20 minutes<br>2 kg/4 lb jars: 30 minutes | 1 kg/2 lb jars: 1 minute<br>2 kg/4 lb jars: 2 minutes |
| Soft berries and currants | Raw pack | Thin – or sprinkle with sugar. Leave overnight and process without further liquid | 1 kg/2 lb jars: 10 minutes<br>2 kg/4 lb jars: 15 minutes | 1 kg/2 lb jars: 1 minute<br>2 kg/4 lb jars: 2 minutes |
| Cherries | Prick each berry to prevent bursting. Raw pack | Heavy | 1 kg/2 lb jars: 20 minutes<br>2 kg/4 lb jars: 30 minutes | 1 kg/2 lb jars: 1 minute<br>2 kg/4 lb jars: 2 minutes |
| Gooseberries | Raw pack | Heavy | 1 kg/2 lb jars: 10 minutes<br>2 kg/4 lb jars: 15 minutes | 1 kg/2 lb jars: 1 minute<br>2 kg/4 lb jars: 2 minutes |
| Rhubarb | Raw pack | Heavy | 1 kg/2 lb jars: 10 minutes<br>2 kg/4 lb jars: 15 minutes | 1 kg/2 lb jars: 1 minute<br>2 kg/4 lb jars: 2 minutes |
| Peaches, halved and stoned | Raw pack | Heavy | 1 kg/2 lb jars: 25 minutes<br>2 kg/4 lb jars: 30 minutes | 1 kg/2 lb jars: 2 minutes<br>2 kg/4 lb jars: 3 minutes |

| | Pack | Liquid | Processing time | Processing time |
|---|---|---|---|---|
| Ripe pears, halved | Raw pack | Medium + squeeze of lemon | 1 kg/2 lb jars: 30 minutes<br>2 kg/4 lb jars: 40 minutes | 1 kg/2 lb jars: 3 minutes<br>2 kg/4 lb jars: 4 minutes |
| Hard pears, whole | Cooked pack | Heavy | 1 kg/2 lb jars: 10 minutes<br>2 kg/4 lb jars: 15 minutes | 1 kg/2 lb jars: 1 minute<br>2 kg/4 lb jars: 2 minutes |
| Plums | Prick to prevent bursting. Raw pack | Heavy or medium | 1 kg/2 lb jars: 20 minutes<br>2 kg/4 lb jars: 25 minutes | 1 kg/2 lb jars: 1 minute<br>2 kg/4 lb jars: 2 minutes |
| Tomatoes, skinned by dipping in boiling water 5 seconds | Raw pack | Salted water with added lemon juice if tomatoes very ripe | 1 kg/2 lb jars: 35 minutes<br>2 kg/4 lb jars: 40 minutes | 1 kg/2 lb jars: 3 minutes<br>2 kg/4 lb jars: 4 minutes |
| Sliced beetroot | Cooked pack | Cooking water with 1 tablespoon vinegar for every 600 ml/1 pint water | 1 kg/2 lb jars: 10 minutes<br>2 kg/4 lb jars: 15 minutes | 1 kg/2 lb jars: 1 minute<br>2 kg/4 lb jars: 2 minutes |
| Mild pickled beetroot (for strong pickled beetroot see Pickles) | Cooked pack | Equal parts cooking water and vinegar (or 75% water, 25% vinegar) | 1 kg/2 lb jars: 10 minutes<br>2 kg/4 lb jars: 15 minutes | 1 kg/2 lb jars: 1 minute<br>0 kg/0 lb jars: 2 minutes |

(Skin only if the skin would be inedible or ugly if candied, e.g. pears or pineapple.) Slice oranges across, skin and all. Canned fruits, being evenly sized and ready-cooked, are simpler to start with than raw fruit. Whole fruits such as figs should be pricked to prevent splitting when boiled.

2. Cook the fruit in water, gently so as not to break them, until tender. (Chestnut skins need to be slit before boiling to facilitate removal, which is easer while they are still hot after 10 minutes' boiling. Scrape off the inner skins too.) Skin angelica stems after cooking.

3. Drain the cooked fruit and put each variety of fruit in a separate bowl.

4. Make a syrup of 1 part water and 3 of granulated sugar (measured by volume) and add a heaped teaspoon of cream of tartar per 600 ml/1 pint to help prevent it crystallising. Stir steadily while bringing to the boil. The sugar should dissolve before the liquid boils.

5. Boil until clear. Pour over the fruit, cover with a piece of cartridge paper with a small hole cut in the middle to let out the steam. Leave 24 hours.

6. Lift the fruit carefully into a clean bowl.

7. Drain the syrup back into the pan, using a rubber spatula to scrape the bowl gently, but take care to leave behind any crystallised sugar, which could start a chain reaction causing all the syrup to crystallise.

8. Boil the syrup, then pour over the fruit again. Repeat this re-boiling and re-soaking until the fruit is clear, shiny and solid to the touch once it is cold. The syrup will be as thick as treacle. This may take 4 days (for redcurrants) or 10 days (for large figs or half pears). If the syrup reduces so that it no longer covers the fruit, additional syrup can be made, but this should be more concentrated – 4 parts sugar to 1 part water plus 1 teaspoon cream of tartar.

The obvious question arises – why not simply leave the fruit in the saucepan of sugar, and re-boil it every day? The answer is that the fruit will get overcooked if this is done. But it is possible, and sensible, to candy hard fruits such as chestnuts in the pan: just re-boil once a day in the syrup without the addition of any extra sugar, until they are glassy-looking.

9. If the fruits are to be stored suspended in sugar syrup, they will keep in glass jars, submerged in their own syrup, for several weeks in a cool place. Refrigerators are too cold, causing the syrup to crystallise to a solid mass.

If the fruits are to be kept longer, they must be packed into preserving jars and processed briefly to sterilise them (see bottling instructions). Suspending in syrup for storage is often done with glacé cherries or chestnuts destined for cooking, where a dry surface is not necessary.

If they are to be packed into boxes they must now be dried.

10. Once the fruit looks and feels ready, lay the pieces on a stainless steel cake rack and leave in a warm kitchen for 2–4 days, until dry to the touch.

11. *If a glacé finish is wanted*, dip the dried fruits one at a time, first in boiling water for a few seconds, then into a hot syrup of 4 parts sugar and 1 of water (the candying syrup may be used if it is still clear and uncrystallised). Leave to dry again. A semi-opaque, slightly flaky glaze should cover each piece.

12. *For a crystallised finish*, dip the fruits one at a time into boiling water, then roll them immediately in caster sugar. Leave to dry again. There is a more complicated professional method of getting a crystallised glaze: lay the dried fruit pieces on a rack or on a tray. Make a syrup of 4 parts sugar and 1 part water (with no added cream of tartar) and allow some of it to wash up the sides of the pan as it boils – tip the pan to do this. This syrup will grain, or form little crystals. Use a wooden spoon to encourage more graining by wetting the pan sides with the syrup, and scraping the crystallised sugar into the syrup. Quite soon the whole pan will be murky with crystals. Spoon the syrup carefully, while hot, over the fruit pieces. The fruit, when dry, will have a fine crystalline crust.

## Crystallised flowers

Suitable flowers are violets, borage (used whole) and geranium or rose petals. Pick perfect, dry flowers, preferably with a vibrant colour. Carefully break large flowers into petals. Separate an egg, putting the white, unwhisked, into a cup. Delicately paint the flower petals with this on both sides. Then dust them lightly and evenly with fine caster sugar, shaking them gently to remove any excess. Lay them on waxed or silicone paper. Allow to dry in a warm, airy room for a day or two until brittle. Store in airtight jars and keep away from the light, which might spoil the colour of the flowers.

# Sponge Cakes

## BARBARA MAHER

Whisked cakes or sponges made a relatively late appearance on the bakery scene, long after pastries and yeast-leavened goods, which were inclined to be on the heavy side. About 1500, a type of sponge biscuit first appeared. This feather-light, aerated combination of eggs and sugar proved to be irresistible, and by the nineteenth century a great majority of cakes were made in a similar way with variations including nuts, fruits, spices and many flavourings.

The sponge mixture also turned out to be a commercial success for the professional bakers. The relatively inexpensive cake could be dressed up in any number of ways, from the most simple to the most elaborate layered and decorated affairs. Eventually that became of paramount importance and the cake itself acted merely as a base made with inferior ingredients. Regrettably that is often still the case.

Sponge cake, so the *Oxford English Dictionary* (1808) informs us, is a 'very light sweet cake made from flour, milk, eggs and sugar'. There is nothing more delicious than a freshly baked home-made sponge cake; but despite the popular familiarity, it still presents a daunting challenge to many – 'I am hopeless at baking' is the common phrase. In face, onct the basic techniques of preparing a sponge have been mastered, you can tackle almost any cake. Choose a quiet time to work, when you can concentrate and not be interrupted; there are no short cuts; accuracy and patience are essential to achieving success and practice makes perfect.

If I am asked what are the three essentials for making a good sponge, my answer is – correct beating of an egg white, careful folding in and an accurate oven. Beating air into a mixture is also a vital factor, and the structure is strengthened by folding in the other ingredients. Lightness, the essence of a good sponge, comes from the eggs in the mixture. The first priority is that the eggs are as fresh as possible; when cracked open, the white should almost hug the egg yolk in a regular circle and disperse very little. If the egg is old, the white will be thin and watery and may even smell slightly stale; it will be difficult to whip up successfully.

An egg white, broken freshly from the shell, is a fluid, translucent and shimmering mass, yet it can be transformed into a white-peaked cloud, more than three times the volume after being whipped for a few minutes. Eggs, and especially the whites, are rather temperamental and must be handled with respect, but once the basic conditions for controlling them are understood, a soufflé, a meringue or a sponge will present little difficulty.

There are two methods of preparing sponge cakes: the first involves beating whole eggs and sugar over simmering water, and the cold method involves whipping the egg whites separately. By the first, more traditional method, the heat speeds up the coagulation of protein in the eggs, allowing large amounts of air to be trapped, and so quickly increases their volume. The sugar dissolves into the warm eggs and gives a finer and smoother texture. This cake is slightly sticky and soft-textured. By the second method, the egg yolks and sugar are beaten in the cold state, and the flour and stiffly beaten egg-white snow are then folded in. Folding in means lightly blending the flour and beaten egg white into the basic mixture with a large metal spoon; this retains the greatest amount of air. Stirring crushes the pockets of air and causes their structure to break down.

At this point the oven (which must be pre-heated) plays its role, for the delicate, aerated sponge mixture must be baked straight away or it will collapse. The heat of the oven encourages the further expansion of the air pockets in the mixture by steam, before the protein in the eggs coagulates with the flour to set the cake. The oven temperature should be accurate, as this too affects the successful rise of the cake, and an oven thermometer is a worthwhile investment if there is any doubt. Try the thermometer in different parts of the oven – not too low or high, depending on where the source of heat is, or the cake may burn – and adjust the thermostat accordingly.

## BAKING A CAKE

**Ingredients.** Use only the best quality ingredients. *Eggs* should be as fresh as possible; the volume produced from fresh whites is far greater than from old eggs. Use *caster sugar* as it liquefies much more quickly when it is heated. Granulated is too coarse. *Flour* should be *plain and soft*. (Strong or hard flour is generally only used for yeasted doughs and cooked choux pastes.)

**What utensils do you need?** You must have a whisk with which to beat both the basic mixture and the egg whites. A large wire balloon whisk is most suitable for hand-beating, where the maximum of air is produced with the minimum of effort. A hand-held electric beater makes for lighter work, but the volume of egg snow is slightly less. An electric table-mixer can be used for beating both the first-stage sponge batter and the egg whites. Ten minutes with the machine set at a medium-high speed will aerate the mixture as well as by hand, but the egg snow will have less volume.

Ideally, you need a round-bottomed large bowl for whisking the batter and for the egg whites. A copper egg-white bowl gives the best result; failing that an enamel or glass bowl is efficient (but add a pinch of salt to help stabilise the whites). Avoid using a plastic bowl, which may be slightly greasy and will inhibit the egg whites' expansion. Egg whites expand to more than three times their original size, so use at least a 25 cm/10 inch bowl for 4 eggs.

Use the largest metal spoon you have for folding in; it cuts through the batter better than a blunter or smaller tool.

If you follow the first method, you need a pan, quarter-filled with water, into which the base of the bowl will fit snugly without touching the water.

A wire rack is also essential because cakes must cool with a current of air all around them, otherwise they become heavy and soggy.

**Which tin?** Always use the size of tin indicated in the recipe: too large a tin will stop the cake rising to its maximum; too small a tin will be too full and the mixture will overflow as it rises. Most suitable is a spring-form tin; this has a clip in the side which springs open to release the base. Or use a tin with a loose base. For a layered sponge, shallow tins with fixed or loose bases can be used, but make sure they are well greased and lined.

**Greasing and lining the tin.** Tins for sponge cakes are best base-lined. The paper ensures that a delicate cake does not stick. Cut a circle of greaseproof or silicone-coated paper, using the base of the tin as template, to fit only the base of the tin. Lightly brush the base and sides with melted, unsalted butter (which has a good flavour); lay the paper in place and brush this with butter too. Shake a mixture of 1 tablespoon caster sugar and 1 tablespoon flour all around the tin, making sure that all the surfaces are coated. This ensures that the cake crust stays soft. Shake off any excess. Avoid over-greasing the tin sides, which makes the cake crusty.

**Prepare the oven.** Cakes must bake in a dry atmosphere; never bake them with other foods which might produce steam and be detrimental to them. Switch on the oven and set it to the correct temperature at least 15 minutes before you need it. Leave it to warm up to gas 4/180° C/350° F.

Baking times are always approximate. Check cakes about 10 minutes before you expect them to be finished.

**Prepare the ingredients.**

1. Leave all the ingredients in the kitchen for at least an hour before you start baking.

2. Weigh out all the ingredients very accurately

3. Sieve the flour very thoroughly to aerate it well. Lift the sieve high up as you shake the flour into a bowl; repeat two or three times.

4. Eggs taken straight out of the refrigerator will be too cold and the volume of the whisked whites will be considerably reduced. Warm eggs briefly if necessary, by placing them in a bowl of warm water for a minute or two.

5. Separate the eggs carefully if you are following the second method. Crack the eggshell on the side of a small bowl and gently prise it apart. Let the egg white fall into the bowl, taking care that none of the yolk passes through (this prevents the white from expanding when it is whipped), and transfer the white to a spotlessly clean whisking bowl. Never crack the egg straight over the whisking bowl, for if you get a bad egg the rest will be spoiled. Put the egg yolk in another mixing bowl. Separate the remaining eggs. Should any yolk fall in, use a half eggshell to scrape it out.

6. Weigh the sugar and disperse or sieve any lumps if necessary.

## PLAIN FATLESS SPONGE

In this basic recipe the flour and sugar each weigh half the weight of the eggs. This sponge keeps fresh for two or three days in an airtight container, or wrapped in aluminium foil.

| 4 whole eggs (200 g/8 oz) | | |
|---|---|---|
| 100 g | 4 oz | caster sugar |
| 100 g | 4 oz | plain soft flour |
| 1 tsp grated lemon zest | | |

*Gas 4/180° C/350° F. Baking time: 30 minutes for a deep cake; 20 minutes for shallow cakes*

## The warmed method

Quarter-fill with water the pan in which your mixing bowl is to rest, and set it on the heat to boil, then turn it down so that the water simmers gently. Break the whole eggs into the mixing bowl and whisk in the sugar lightly. Set the bowl over the water, making sure that the underside does not touch the water, otherwise the eggs will cook and the mixture overheat. The aim is simply to help the protein in the eggs coagulate and develop volume quickly.

**The ribbon stage.** Continue whisking the eggs and sugar together. After a while the mixture starts to change in colour and volume. It turns from a rich, shiny, egg-yellow colour to a pale lemon shade and loses its coarse, grainy texture to become rather dense and fluffy (not unlike mayonnaise). It will at least double in bulk. At this point (which takes about 20 minutes by hand and 10 by machine), when a little of the beaten egg mixture is allowed to fall from the whisk back into the bowl, it will leave a *ribbon trail* on the surface for 2 or 3 seconds before it disappears. Draw the bowl off he heat and continue whisking whilst it cools and thickens. Whisk in the lemon zest.

**Folding in by hand.** Flour must be folded in by hand, so as to retain the maximum amount of the air which has been developed in the mixture and which is essential for achieving a good rise to the cake. Use a metal spoon.

Sift a small amount of flour across the egg and sugar surface; cut down through the mixture in a figure-of-eight movement, round and out and high into the air (this also helps aerate). Rotate the mixing bowl between flour additions so that the mixture is combined evenly with the flour. When all the flour has been used, pour the mixture into the prepared 22–24 cm/9–10 inch lined cake tin or divide it between two shallow sandwich tins. Lightly smooth the surface, then rap the tin sharply on the work surface once to disperse any air bubbles, and place immediately in the pre-heated oven.

## The separated egg method

In this method the maximum of air is produced from the egg whites by beating them separately. The basic mixture is not warmed.

Use the same ingredients as in the first method, but carefully separate the eggs first. (See note 5, p. 99). Reserve 2 tablespoonfuls of sugar and whisk the remainder with the egg yolks in a large mixing bowl, by hand, with a hand-held mixer or in the bowl of an electric table-mixer. When the mixture has turned to a pale, creamy lemon colour and reached the thick ribbon stage (see previous method) after about 20 minutes' beating by hand or 10 by machine, stir in the lemon zest and set aside whilst you beat the egg whites. This mixture will keep quite well for a short while without spoiling.

**How to handle egg whites.** There is no way of retrieving a collapsed, whisked egg white, so you must prevent this happening. The following points will help:

1. Once you start beating the egg white, continue until it has fully expanded – do not stop mid-way or it will collapse.

2. When the beaten white is ready, use it immediately, for the aerated state will hold firm for only a minute or two before it starts to disintegrate. (When sugar is beaten in, it holds its peaks a little longer.)

3. Prepare the host mixture (yolks and sugar) first, so that

it is ready to accept the beaten egg white immediately.

4. Always *fold* in beaten white *by hand*; never stir it.

5. Use a metal spoon for folding in, the sharp, thin edge cuts through the mixture more efficiently.

**Whisking the egg white.** Pour the egg white into the copper egg-white bowl. Use the large balloon whisk or the hand-held electric mixer. (A table-mixer will beat egg white fairly well, but cannot really incorporate enough air. An electric food processor is completely unsuitable.)

Start beating slowly at first until the white begins to froth, then more vigorously. As you beat, lift the tool up out of the bowl, and back down through the mixture in a figure of eight (just as with folding in) making sure that all comes across its path. The mass will then start to thicken, become dense and form into soft but firm snowy peaks. It will have at least trebled in volume. *Stop now*. You should be able to turn the bowl upside down and the snow should remain intact. If you beat longer, the mixture will start to separate, become coarse, slightly grainy and water, and eventually collapse. There is no way of retrieving it.

Beat in the two reserved tablespoonfuls of sugar until the mixture looks glossy, satiny and smooth. It takes just a few seconds.

**Folding in.** Whisked egg white is folded into the yolk and sugar mixture in the same way as flour, and as the flour also has to be folded in, alternate the two. First lighten the yolk mixture by mixing 2 tablespoonfuls of egg snow into it, then sift part of the flour across the surface and fold it in using the metal spoon, followed by more egg white. Fold in lightly and carefully, remembering to retain as much air as possible. Continue folding alternate siftings of flour and whisked egg white until all is used up. Pour the mixture into the prepared tin or tins, smooth the surface, then rap the tin sharply on the work top once, and place immediately in the oven.

**Testing the cake for readiness.** Since oven temperatures vary slightly, baking times must be approximate. Always check a cake 10 minutes or so before the completed cooking period, but never before at least three quarters of the baking time has passed, because a sudden draught or gust of cold air will cause the cake to collapse. Ease the oven door open very carefully and close it with as much consideration.

A well cooked sponge should have risen almost to fill the tin, should be slightly domed and golden coloured – the eggs give the rich colour. It should feel slightly springy to the touch and be shrinking away a little from the walls of the cake tin. If you are still uncertain, gently pierce the middle of the cake with a warmed metal skewer, or a wooden toothpick: it should come out quite clean with no cake batter adhering. Leave in the oven a few minutes more if necessary.

Lift the cake out of the oven and set it down carefully on a wire rack. A cooling cake should always have air circulating freely around it or it will be soggy. Leave to settle for 5 minutes, then run a knife around the inner edge of the tin to release the cake before pulling back the clip of the tin and lifting away the ring. Place a second rack or thin, flat board on top of the cake and quickly invert it all so that the sheet of lining paper and the base of the tin can be removed. Turn the cake back over onto the wire rack to cool; or if the cake is to be iced, turn the bottom side to the top as it has a smoother and flatter surface.

## What can you do with a plain sponge cake?

For a tea-time treat, split in half and spread the base of the sponge with 3 tablespoons of a sharp-flavoured jam, and smother with 150 ml/¼ pint stiffly whipped, lightly sweetened double cream. Sandwich with the lid and dredge with icing sugar.

Try home-made lemon curd for a change; for this you will

need to flavour the basic sponge mixture first with 2 teaspoons of grated lemon zest – never add juice (unless a recipe tells you to) as this can have a disastrous effect on the mixture and make it soggy.

Fresh soft fruits, such as strawberries, raspberries and redcurrants, are especially attractive and taste delicious with whipped cream in a fresh sponge. Sprinkle kirsch or sherry onto the cake to give an extra punch.

## A simple chocolate sponge

Assemble the basic ingredients (p. 100). In addition you need: 1 teaspoon instant coffee powder and 1 tablespoon cocoa powder sifted with the flour in the basic recipe; 60 g/ 2 oz plain, dark dessert chocolate, finely grated; 1½ teaspoons bicarbonate of soda dissolved in a tablespoon of milk and set aside.

Beat the chocolate into the aerated egg and sugar mixture. Fold the milk and bicarbonate through the finished mixture. Bake as usual. Split the cold cake and fill with chocolate- and coffee-flavoured whipped cream.

If you prefer to flavour the sponge with cocoa rather than chocolate replace between a quarter and a half of the flour in the recipe with unsweetened cocoa powder (not milk drinking chocolate which is very bland and too sweet). Sift well together with the flour and proceed as before.

### GENOESE SPONGE

When melted and cooled butter is added to the fatless sponge mixture it is known as *genoese*. This sponge is commonly used in the bakery trade and serves as a basis for *petits fours*, and both simple and elaborate layered cakes and gâteaux. Butter improves the keeping qualities and the sponge will stay fresh for up to a week. Like fatless sponges, it freezes very successfully (see p. 110). The best genoese is made with equal parts of flour, sugar and butter, whilst a less rich version uses half the amount of butter.

Use unsalted butter which has a sweeter flavour or good-quality slightly salted butter. Never use margarine, which has no flavour at all.

If you lightly brown the butter whilst melting (take care not to burn it), the cake will have a slightly nutty taste.

The basic method for preparing the sponge cake is the same as before and either process, whether the warmed or the cold method, can be used. The cooled melted butter is folded in alternately with the flour and beaten egg white to finish.

## A rich genoese sponge

| 4 whole eggs (200 g/8 oz) | | |
|---|---|---|
| 120 g | 4½ oz | caster sugar |
| 120 g | 4½ oz | plain soft flour |
| 120 g | 4½ oz | unsalted butter |
| 1 tsp lemon zest or | | |
| 1 tbs liqueur (rum or kirsch) | | |
| Gas 4/180° C/350° F. Baking time: 45 minutes | | |

Melt the butter slowly in a small pan. (Leave to brown lightly for a nutty flavour.) Set aside to cool. Follow either the warmed method (p. 100) or the separated egg method (p. 101). Fold in the melted butter alternately with the flour (and egg white if using second method). Take care, as you add the butter, not to let any of the rather grainy deposit lying in the bottom of the pan fall in.

Continue folding in until the flour, butter and egg white (if appropriate) are used up. Pour the finished batter quickly into the prepared (p. 98) 22–24 cm/9–10 inch tins and bake immediately in the pre-heated oven.

A genoese sponge can be filled with a rich butter cream that has been flavoured with orange or lemon or with a liqueur. Ground almonds, hazelnuts or walnuts, chocolate and coffee are also good. Cover the cake with the same cream, or coat with a suitable glacé icing.

## BISCUIT DE SAVOIE

In France a sponge is known as *biscuit,* and the *biscuit de Savoie* probably originated there sometime during the latter half of the seventeenth century. For many decades it was considered to be very special and offered at festivities and for celebrations. Although it is made with the same basic ingredients as the simple fat-free sponge – sugar, flour and eggs – the proportions vary. Icing sugar is used because it is lighter, and half the plain flour is replaced by potato flour. Potato flour is made from potatoes that have been boiled and dried; its texture is very dense but light and it has a distinctive, rather sweet, creamy flavour.

The biscuit is quite different from an ordinary sponge – delicate, rather short and dry. It crumbles easily and 'melts' in the mouth. It is coloured a pale lemon and will keep fresh for up to a week.

Do not substitute cornflour for potato flour; even though the baked properties might be similar, it has almost no flavour at all.

Be careful if using flower water; it is very strongly perfumed and too much will spoil the cake's flavour.

## *Biscuit de Savoie*

The separated egg method (p. 101) is used for preparation. Use a slightly larger tin – 24–26 cm/10–11 inches.

| 70 g | $2\frac{1}{2}$ oz | *plain soft flour* |
|------|------|------|
| 70 g | $2\frac{1}{2}$ oz | *potato flour* |
| 6 *egg yolks* | | |
| 200 g | 7 oz | *icing sugar* |

| |
|---|
| 1 *tbs vanilla sugar* or |
| ½ *tsp orange flower water* or |
| 1 *tbs Grand Marnier or Cointreau* |
| 5 *egg whites* |
| *a pinch of salt* |
| 3 *tsp lemon juice* |
| *Gas 4/180° C/350° F. Baking time: approx 30 minutes* |

Sift the flours together two or three times and aerate well. Whisk the egg yolks and all but 2 tablespoons of sugar until the thick ribbon stage has been reached (see p. 100). Sift a third of the flour mixture across the surface and lightly fold it in using a large metal spoon. In the same way fold in the rest of the flour and the flavouring. Beat the egg white in another bowl (with a pinch of salt unless it is made of copper) until it stands in firm, snowy peaks. Sift the two tablespoons of reserved sugar over and whisk it in until the meringue is smooth and slightly shiny. Fold in the lemon juice.

Mix two tablespoons of meringue into the sugar and egg yolk mixture to lighten it, then, using a metal spoon, gently fold in the remainder in two or three stages. Pour immediately into the prepared (p. 98) cake tin and bake in the pre-heated oven.

## ROULADE AND SPONGE ROLL

A thin sheet of sponge cake rolled up with a filling inside is a handsome alternative to the more conventional round shape. Jam, whipped double cream, fresh soft fruits, and nut, or chocolate- and coffee-flavoured butter creams can be used. The outside of the roll can be dressed up elaborately with melted chocolate or cream and decorated or it can simply be dredged with sugar.

All of the sponge recipes are suitable; the basic fatless sponge is ideal for the simple, eat-at-once cakes, whilst the genoese and *biscuit de Savoie*, with their longer keeping characteristics, are preferable for richer fillings.

A thin layer of baked sponge must be rolled whilst still hot, for as it cools it crisps and hardens. With a jam filling this is no problem for it can be rolled with the cake whilst it is still warm but all other fillings which might melt or spoil must be used when the cake has cooled down. In this case the cake must be rolled *unfilled*, whilst still warm.

**Which tin? How to grease and line it.** For a successful sponge roll it is essential to line the baking sheet with paper. Greaseproof, silicone-coated, or aluminium foil (which I find most efficient) should be used.

Use a 25 × 36 × 1 cm/10 × 14½ × ½ inch rectangular Swiss roll baking tin.

Cut the paper a little larger than the tin. Brush the baking sheet with melted, unsalted butter and line it with the paper, making sure that it lies smoothly, and folding in the corners lightly if necessary. Leave the extra paper over-hanging the sides. Carefully brush the lining paper with more melted butter. (Unsalted butter helps stop the cake sticking to the paper.)

The oven temperature must be hotter for a thin sponge, and the baking time is much shorter.

Pre-heat the oven to gas 8/230°C/450°F.

## Roulade au biscuit de Savoie

I find this sponge the most suitable for the technique. The lining paper can be peeled off the cake much more readily than is the case with the others, because the sponge crisps slightly less than the other two as it cools, which means that it is less inclined to split or crack as it is rolled. Use half the basic recipe ingredients to make one roulade to fit the tin specified above.

| 40 g | 1½ oz | plain soft flour |
|------|-------|------------------|
| 40 g | 1½ oz | potato flour |

| | | |
|---|---|---|
| 3 egg yolks | | |
| 100 g | 3½ oz | icing sugar |
| 3 small egg whites | | |
| 2 tsp vanilla sugar or | | |
| 2–3 drops orange flower water or | | |
| 1 tbs Grand Marnier or Cointreau | | |
| 1½ tsp lemon juice | | |

Prepare the sponge mixture by the separated egg method (p. 101) and pour it straight into the lined baking sheet. Gently smooth the mixture and ease it into all the corners with a spatula, and take care not to break down the aerated structure. Bake in the hot oven immediately.

*The baking time is no more than 10 or 12 minutes* – if you over-bake it it will become hard, crisp and biscuity and impossible to roll.

The cake will rise well, feel slightly springy to the touch – but less so than a conventional sponge – and be golden in colour.

Whilst the sponge is baking, prepare for the next stage. Lay a clean tea towel on the work surface, cover it with a sheet of greaseproof or silicone-coated paper, cut a little wider and longer than the roulade and dredge liberally with caster sugar. As soon as the cake is ready, lift it out of the oven and turn it straight over onto the sugared paper. Peel off the baking paper very carefully, so that the cake does not tear – moisten the paper edges very slightly with water if they stick. Trim away the crisp, uneven edges of cake with a sharp knife.

**For a jam roll,** the sponge can be rolled up with a warm jam filling. Spread 5 or 6 tablespoons of warmed jam (add a tablespoon of water to make it smoother if need be) to within 1 cm/½ inch of the cake edge.

**How to roll it up.** Using the tea towel and sugared paper as a guide, start rolling from the short side. Tuck the first turn in neatly and firmly across the width, then roll more lightly as you continue. (The sugar on the paper stops the outside getting damaged.) Make sure that the cake join lies underneath and place it on a wire rack; leave to cool. Dredge with icing sugar before serving.

**For a cream- or fruit-filled roulade,** invert the hot sponge onto the sugared paper and peel off the baking paper as before; trim away the edges.

Cover the sponge with a second, clean sheet of greaseproof paper, and roll the cake up, with the paper inside, using the towel to ease it into a loose roll. Lay on the wire rack to cool, with the join underneath, but cover the cake with a slightly damp cloth. This ensures that the sponge stays moist and more pliable, making it easier to roll later.

When it has cooled completely, unroll carefully so as not to damage it; fill with the filling, roll up, and decorate.

### FREEZING NOTES

It is always best to freeze ready-baked sponge cakes, undecorated and unfilled. Stand the cake on paper or polythene on a flat board or tray and freeze uncovered. When it has frozen, wrap carefully in aluminium foil, a plastic freezer bag or suitable plastic container and seal carefully.

A fatless sponge keeps well for 9–10 months; a genoese – with fat – stays fresh for only 4 months.

Defrost whilst still wrapped, at room temperature for an hour or so. Then fill and decorate as required.

## *Here are the main points again*

1. You need peace and quiet to concentrate. Follow the instructions precisely.

2. Ingredients should be warmed to room temperature

before being weighed out very carefully and accurately. Sift flour well to aerate; separate eggs.

3. Pre-heat the oven to the correct temperature.

4. Grease and line the tins of the stated size so that the mixture can be turned straight into them as soon as it is ready.

5. Bake the cake immediately in the warmed oven.

6. Do not open the oven door until at least three quarters of the cooking time has passed. Do not bang the oven door.

7. Test for readiness with a warmed skewer; the cake should be slightly domed, shrinking from the sides of the tin and golden brown.

8. Cool the cake on a wire rack where the air can circulate round it, otherwise it will be heavy and soggy.

9. The cake must be quite cool before it is iced or filled (unless it is a jam roulade).

10. Store in an airtight tin, wrapped in aluminium foil or plastic film when cold.

11. Never put a warm cake in the refrigerator or freezer. Wait until it has cooled down completely.

## What went wrong? — Some possible faults

Even the most practised baker will experience problems at one time or another; so what went wrong?

**A damp and heavy cake with a sunken top:** too small a tin; too cool an oven; a sudden draught before the cake has set properly; the oven door slammed shut; too short a baking time.

**A badly cracked cake surface:** too much mixture in the tin; too hot an oven; cake set too high in the oven.

**Cake texture too coarse:** wrong sugar; not enough whisking of eggs with sugar; too cool an oven.

**Cake not brown enough:** not baked long enough or oven overloaded, which prevents heat circulating properly.

**Base burned and cake top too brown:** incorrect lining of tin; cake set too low in oven; too large a tin so that layer of mixture is too thin; oven too hot.

# Sauces

## ANTON MOSIMANN

Sauce is one of those French words which came into the English language with the advent of the Normans and have remained unchanged to this day. A sauce is still a liquid or soft relish designed to make our food more appetising. In medieval household accounts 'salt and sauce' are most often shown as a single entry, a strong indication that sauces were mostly, if not exclusively, savoury relishes used to make fish and meat more palatable, no doubt often to disguise what they had suffered in transit or storage. Present-day refrigeration and rapid transport have banished the need to sauce over those unpleasant reminders that most foodstuffs are highly perishable. Sauces are no longer a disguise, but a way to make food look better, smell better, taste better, to make it at the same time more appetising and more nutritious.

These two approaches to the use of sauces are reflected in the existence of two schools, that of Carême and that of Escoffier. Among the faithful, in the great kitchens of the world, Escoffier is to Carême what the New Testament is to the Old.

Antonin Carême (1784–1833) and his disciples produced sauces that were works of art, beautiful, delicious, but complicated. Their chief concern might well have been, indeed probably was, camouflage. Many of the sauces he used or introduced were strong and spicy: *vert-pré* (mayonnaise with a purée of green herbs), *périgueux* (a *demi-glace* with truffles), *matelote* and *bourguignotte* (both for fish), *aigre-doux, piquante, salmis* (for game birds), *Robert* (mustard), *raifort* (horseradish) and so on. Of course there were others, such as the *sauce suprême* and the *hollandaise* which have kept their position among the favourite classics, but on the whole Carême sauces killed rather than helped bring out the natural flavour of the meat, game, fish or poultry with which they were served.

Grimod de la Reynière, a contemporary of both Carême and Brillat-Savarin, and author of the *Almanach des Gourmands*, rather overstated the case for this class of sauces when he vowed 'I would eat my own father with such a sauce.' His father, the son of a pork butcher, might have found this a dubious statement. Auguste Escoffier (1847–1935) took a different view. He was the apostle of simplicity who wanted his sauces to help and not to hide the essential flavour of whatever dish they adorned. He introduced, and had the greatest faith in, *fumets* and *essences*: evaporated stock obtained by allowing the water, milk, or wine in which meat, fish or vegetables happen to be cooked, to steam away slowly so as to reduce to a fragrant concentrate which he would then use as the basis for the sauce that was to be served with the dish.

The old French proverb 'c'est la sauce qui fait manger le poisson' would be regarded with grave suspicion by the Escoffier school. Fish that cannot be eaten unless it be buried under a camouflage sauce had better be buried altogether, but the delicate flavour of a fresh Dover sole cooked in white wine is enhanced, not blurred, by a sauce made from the greatly reduced cooking liquid.

The main difference between the old and the new schools is inherent in the base on which most sauces are constructed: the flour-based sauces (*roux brun* and *blond,* or *espagnole* and *allemande* as they are called after their complexion rather than their origin) are less and less popular now, and the great favourites of the day are delicate, light, easily digestible *fumets* and *essences*.

A good chef is recognised by his sauces. In the orchestra

of a large kitchen, the *saucier* is a soloist and it is a fact that the position of *saucier* is suitable only for a keen and experienced person. On the other hand, there is no longer any excuse for the deep-rooted Anglo-Saxon suspicion that the making of a successful sauce is an extremely complicated process fraught with difficulties and gallic fiendishness. Most of the classic French sauces are well within the understanding and achievement of any interested cook anywhere in the world. The few really complicated ones are better left alone, or ordered in a restaurant which happens to offer them.

## THE PRINCIPLES OF SAUCE-MAKING

The variety of sauces is the basic wealth of a good cuisine. The quality of a sauce is determined by its colour, texture and consistency and it should have a good shine. Natural flavours should predominate, but the taste must not be too strong or it will overwhelm the flavour of the food it accompanies.

It may be fanciful to call a good appetite the best sauce of all, but certainly some sauces are of the utmost simplicity, and though few of us would think of plain meat gravy as a sauce, it is as good a relish as any roast requires. Two of the simplest sauces are melted butter (an emollient) and mint sauce (a stimulant). The majority of sauces, however, are a combination of various elements, affording the cook a chance to display an individual touch even while adhering to the main directions laid down in cookery books.

The basis of most sauces is some nourishing substance such as cream or milk, butter or oil, or an 'essence', a concentrated meat, fish or vegetable stock. The consistency of the sauce is determined by various binding or thickening agents, principally egg yolks, flour and related starches such as potato flour (*fécule*), cornflour and arrowroot, and butter, cream or other dairy products such as yogurt, *fromage blanc* etc., or a combination of these ingredients. Blood may also be used, particularly for game dishes. Flavouring agents include herbs, spices, wines and juices. These three groups of ingredients permit endless permutations of colour, flavour and consistency.

Despite the limitless variations in taste and appearance, the foundations upon which sauces are constructed are very few and they have changed but little. The key to the different families of sauces is the type of binding agent used and the way it is incorporated, in other words the type of *liaison*. There are two basic liaison principles on which the majority of traditional sauces are based.

## The roux principle

This makes use of flour mixed with butter, a mixture that is capable of binding roughly 100 ml of liquid for every 30 g of its own weight (a quarter of a pint to each ounce).

In its simplest form, as white or blond roux, the lightly cooked butter and flour mixture is the basis of three of the foundation sauces: *béchamel* in which the liquid used is milk, *velouté* in which the liquid is a white stock (whether of meat, fish or vegetables), and *allemande* which is a thick *velouté* enriched with egg yolks and cream.

Cooking the roux mixture further (not necessarily using butter, but often pork fat or fat in which something else has been cooked) until it is an even brown colour makes a brown roux from which the fourth of the foundation sauces is obtained, the *espagnole*, made with brown stock. Adding meat jelly to the *espagnole* results in a *demi-glace*.

## The emulsion principle

This principle underlies the two remaining foundation sauces. In this process egg yolks are used to absorb and hold in suspension a quantity of oil (in *mayonnaise*, the basis of most cold sauces) or butter (in *hollandaise*). One egg yolk will cope with up to 100 g/4 oz of butter, 250 ml/½ pint of oil, but it is safer not to go for the maximum.

A last and lesser family based on the emulsion principle is the *vinaigrette* group, but these are not really stable sauces, as the oil is only held in temporary suspension in vinegar.

## Other liaisons

**Beurre manié** or kneaded butter is made by blending flour and butter in the proportion of one third flour to two thirds butter. It is added in little bits to the simmering sauce towards the end of the cooking time. The sauce must be stirred all the time with a whisk and will thicken very quickly.

**An uncooked starch**. If a sauce seems too thin it can be thickened by adding a little potato flour (*fécule*) blended with cold water. The liquid must be boiling as the potato flour mixture is added and it must be stirred rapidly.

**Egg yolks**. Beat up egg yolks in a large bowl and add a large spoonful of the hot sauce to them. Stir well until amalgamated, then add a further spoonful and stir in. Return this mixture to the hot sauce and whisk over moderate heat. On no account must it boil or the eggs will curdle.

**Blood**. Blood is used to thicken game sauces, following the method used for egg yolks. Once again the thickening sauce must not be allowed to boil.

**Butter, cream or cream cheese**. Add small nuts of butter, teaspoons of cream or cream cheese to the hot sauce, swirling the pan round and round as they dissolve. These liaisons will thicken and enrich the sauce.

### STOCKS AND ESSENCES

A well prepared stock forms the best base for a good sauce.

By reducing the stock to an essence we can obtain a stronger sauce which is finished with cream or butter. It may then be beaten or bound with a further liaison to make it lighter.

The careful preparation of the broth is an absolute necessity in the making of good soups, sauces, and indeed many other dishes. With bone broths, only fresh bones should be used and these should be broken into small pieces beforehand to obtain all the goodness from them. Bones that are not quite so fresh should be washed and blanched first. Frozen bones can be used.

The longer a stock is cooked (except fish stock) the stronger the taste will be.

To make a *meat extract*, a brown stock is used. This is strained into a small saucepan and then reduced until a shiny, dark brown, thick extract is produced. It should be put into earthenware pots, covered with foil and stored for later use. The extract is used to strengthen various sauces, to flavour *béarnaise* sauce and with white meat or fish dishes.

## Poultry broth

| |
|---|
| 1½ kg/3 lb poultry bones (also cleaned stomach, neck and heart) |
| 1– 2 onions |
| 1 carrot |
| 1 small leek |
| 1 piece of celeriac |
| 1 clove |
| 1 bay leaf |
| 6 crushed peppercorns |
| 1 small sprig of thyme |
| water |

Cut the prepared vegetables coarsely. Crush the poultry bones and put into a large pan. Add cold water and bring to the boil slowly. Skim off the fat and only now add the vegetables and herbs and cook the broth over a gentle heat for 2–3 hours. Skim off the fat from the surface. Then strain the stock through a sieve, allow to cool and skim again.

Use for white or pale sauces (fricassees, blanquettes), some soups.

## Brown veal broth

| |
|---|
| *2–3 kg/4–6 lb chopped veal bones* |
| *1 small piece of veal trotter* |
| *fat or oil for roasting* |
| *1 piece of celeriac* |
| *2 large onions* |
| *some parsley stalks* |
| *1 bay leaf* |
| *1 clove* |
| *3 tbs tomato purée* |
| *water* |

Brown the bones and trotter in a roasting tin (preferably a cast-iron one) in a hot oven for ten minutes and then roast more slowly in a little oil. Add the chopped vegetables and roast them for ten minutes and then mix well with the tomato purée. Add some water and reduce it almost completely to ensure that the broth has a good colour. Then add enough water to cover everything and boil the broth slowly for about 4 hours. Do not cover. Skim occasionally. Then strain the broth through a sieve and reduce according to taste.

A *glace de viande* is obtained when this strained broth is reduced to a thick consistency, about one tenth of the original volume.

Use for brown sauces and for dishes served in their own sauce such as *coq au vin* or a *ragoût*.

## Game broth

Preparation as above, using finely chopped bones of game. Include a few juniper berries.

# Fish broth

| |
|---|
| 1 kg/2 lb sole or turbot bones |
| 1–2 onions |
| 1 small piece of celeriac |
| 1 piece of leek |
| 3 parsley stalks |
| a few mushroom stalks (optional) |
| water |

Wash the fish bones and break into rough pieces. Sweat in butter with the coarsely chopped vegetables without giving them any colour. Add the water so that everything is covered and cook the stock over a low heat for 30 minutes. Pass through a sieve.

# Fish fumet

Proceed in the same way, but this time add fish stock instead of water.

## ROUX-THICKENED SAUCES

These sauces begin with a roux, or thickening mixture or fat and flour. There are three different types of roux.

# Roux blanc (white roux)

Melt the butter in a saucepan of convenient size, blend in the flour and cook gently for a while. The roux should be smooth, but should not be allowed to colour.

# Roux blond (light brown roux)

The ingredients are the same as for the white roux. Cooking must be done very slowly and discontinued as soon as the roux begins to turn colour.

## Roux brun (brown roux)

The mixture of butter and flour is cooked slowly until it is nut-brown in colour.

**Potato flour (fécule).** Rather than using ordinary flour in the preparation of certain delicate sauces, some cooks like to use potato flour. When this is used, sauces need to simmer less long and, as a consequence, do not tend to become over-salted as is sometimes the case when ordinary flour is used; further, the sauce looks more transparent and 'stands up' better when made with *fécule*. Once ready, a *fécule*-made sauce should not remain too long on the heat or it will become too clear in appearance. Cornflour and arrowroot may also be used in place of flour.

**Adding the liquid.** Allow the roux to cool a little, then gradually add the hot liquid, whisking all the time to prevent lumps forming. Bring back to the boil and simmer for twenty minutes; the sauce will become lighter during cooking.

**Proportions.** For a thin or pouring sauce use 30 g/1 oz butter and the same amount of flour to $\frac{1}{2}$ litre/1 pint of liquid. For a thicker, coating sauce use twice as much flour and butter.

## The basic sauces

With the information above you can make *béchamel* (white roux and milk), *velouté* (blond roux plus white stock) and *espagnole* (brown roux and brown stock). For a rich blond sauce use thin cream instead of milk. For *sauce allemande*, a thick velouté enriched with egg yolks and cream, use 2 yolks, 150 ml/$\frac{1}{4}$ pint cream to $\frac{1}{2}$ litre/1 pint sauce. Follow the instructions for the egg yolk liaison on p. 117.

## *Some problems with roux-thickened sauces*

| Fault | Reasons | Corrections and comments |
|---|---|---|
| Tastes floury | 1. Roux insufficiently cooked out<br>2. Roux and stock not mixed well in first instance | 1. Cook roux carefully until taste is right<br>2. Add the stock to the roux a little at a time; make sure it is well emulsified before adding more |
| Tastes bitter | Roux was burnt or stock was bitter in the first place | Watch roux carefully whilst cooking; if the stock is bitter there is no remedy: start again |
| Dull sauce, no shine | Sauce not skimmed during cooking, therefore scum on top is boiled into sauce | Essential to skim sauces frequently to clarify them |
| Wrong colour | 1. Stock wrong colour to begin with<br>2. Roux not cooked to right degree for sauce (too pale, too dark) | No remedy<br><br>Start again, and pay more attention to cooking roux |
| Wrong consistency | 1. Wrong amount of flour or liquid<br>2. Roux is overcooked: starch changes chemically and loses its thickening properties | (See below)<br><br>Avoid overcooking; check consistency of sauces before leaving the kitchen |
| Lumpy | Roux badly mixed | Force through a sieve, then simmer |
| Too thick | Insufficient liquid | Thin with stock (*velouté*) or milk (*béchamel*) |
| Too thin | Too much liquid | Reduce over moderate heat whilst stirring or add a thickening agent |

## HOT EMULSION SAUCES

Hot emulsion sauces, or beaten sauces, are butter sauces to which no flour is added to bind them. The liaison is achieved by beating together egg yolk and butter over gentle heat, preferably in a double boiler. When egg yolks are added to a sauce, they should be beaten with a teaspoonful of cold water and then a little of the sauce stirred into the yolks. Remove the pan from the heat and stir the mixture into the rest of the sauce by degrees. Stir until well blended. Return to the double boiler. Stir constantly until thick, but do not allow to boil or the sauce will curdle.

Sauces which have been made with eggs and butter should be kept moderately warm in a *bain-marie*. If they become too warm there is a danger that they will curdle. Should this happen, in order to save the sauce pour a few drops of water on to one spot in the saucepan and, using a whisk, stir the surface carefully on that same spot with a circular movement until the liaison is restored. Then gradually the circles can be increased until the sauce is quite smooth. It is best not to keep these sauces waiting for more than an hour or two. Left over *hollandaise* can be refrigerated for a few days and used to enrich *béchamels* or *veloutés*. If you intend to use it again as *hollandaise*, beat two tablespoons of the sauce in the top of a double boiler, over hot water. Gradually add the rest of the sauce.

## *Sauce hollandaise*

| | | |
|---|---|---|
| 50 ml | 2 fl oz | white wine |
| 3 tbs white wine vinegar | | |
| 5 crushed white peppercorns | | |
| 1–2 chopped shallots or 1 chopped onion | | |
| 3 parsley stalks | | |
| 2–3 egg yolks | | |
| 350 g | 12 oz | butter |
| salt | | |
| 2 drops of lemon juice | | |
| a pinch of cayenne pepper | | |

Mix together the white wine, vinegar, crushed pepper-corns, shallots or onion and parsley stalks and reduce to 3 tablespoons of liquid. Strain the reduction into an oven-proof dish, pressing out the onions well.

Add the egg yolks to the cooled reduction and whisk to a creamy consistency over a lightly simmering *bain-marie*. Now pour in the warm melted butter, at the same time stirring slowly. Season the sauce with salt, lemon juice and cayenne pepper.

## Sauce maltaise

This is *hollandaise* sauce with much-reduced orange juice and blanched strips of orange. Used particularly for asparagus.

## Sauce mousseline

Just before serving the *hollandaise* sauce, add some whip-ped cream.

## Sauce béarnaise

This is *sauce hollandaise* with tarragon. Use tarragon vinegar instead of white wine vinegar and tarragon stalks instead of parsley stalks and at the end add some chopped fresh tarragon.

## Some problems with hot emulsion sauces

| Fault | Reasons | Corrections and comments |
|---|---|---|
| Egg yolks become too thick | Temperature too high | Add a few drops of cold water |
| Egg yolks do not become thick and creamy | Temperature too low | Increase heat a little |

| Fault | Reasons | Corrections and comments |
|-------|---------|--------------------------|
| Curdles | 1. Butter added too hot | Put a little boiling water in a bowl and gradually incorporate the curdled sauce |
| | 2. Sauce kept too warm during service | Put the sauce in a warm, not hot part of the service area |
| | 3. Equipment not properly washed | |
| Lumpy | Eggs cooked carelessly so they scramble | Careful whisking of eggs away from direct heat is essential; if eggs scramble the only solution is to start again |

## COLD EMULSION SAUCES

Mayonnaise is the sauce on which many cold sauces are based. These can be stored for a longer period, but should not be kept so cold that the oil curdles and the sauce has to be beaten up again from the beginning.

The recipe and method for making mayonnaise are given by Elizabeth David on p. 48.

## Sauce rémoulade

Add chopped capers, tarragon, parsley and anchovy fillet to mayonnaise.

## Aïoli

Pounded garlic is added to the egg yolk before the oil is added.

## Some problems with cold emulsion sauces

| Fault | Reasons | Corrections and comments |
| --- | --- | --- |
| Too thick | Yolks may vary in size; too much oil may have been added | Add a little warm water and vinegar; well made sauce should keep its shape when heaped on a spoon |
| Curdles | Ingredients too cold or not enough attention to blending | Start again with a fresh egg yolk in a clean bowl and add curdled sauce a little at a time |

SAUCES THICKENED WITH BUTTER, CREAM ETC.

## Beurre blanc

(White butter)

| 3 chopped shallots | | |
| --- | --- | --- |
| 3 crushed peppercorns | | |
| 250 ml | 8 fl oz | white wine |
| 1 tbs cream | | |
| 150 g | 5 oz | butter |
| salt | | |
| 2 drops of lemon juice or sherry vinegar | | |

Reduce the chopped shallots, crushed peppercorns and white wine to 50 ml/2 oz of liquid. Strain, pressing out the shallots well.

Allow the reduction to cool a little, whisk in the soft butter, in flakes, and the cream over low heat. Do not let the butter melt completely; the sauce must become thick and creamy. Season with salt, lemon juice or sherry vinegar and flavour with chives, fresh chervil or basil depending on what it will be used for.

*To vary*, reduce the shallots without the peppercorns and then do not strain but leave them in the sauce.

This sauce goes well with fish or shellfish dishes, vegetable flans or vegetable terrines.

## Sauce crème moderne

| 50 ml | 2 fl oz | dry white wine |
|---|---|---|
| 10 g | 2 tsp | finely chopped shallots |
| 80 g | 3 oz | finely chopped mushrooms |
| finely chopped tarragon | | |
| salt and pepper | | |
| 80 ml | 2½ fl oz | fish stock |
| 30 g | 1 oz | cream cheese |

Reduce the white wine to a quarter of its original volume. Add the shallots, mushrooms and tarragon. Season with salt and pepper. Cover and allow to simmer for 2 minutes. Add the fish stock, boil up again and add the cream cheese. Keep moderately warm until needed.

Excellent with fish and vegetable dishes.

## Chive, chervil or tarragon sauce

| 200 ml | 7 fl oz | dry white wine |
|---|---|---|
| 1 bunch chopped chives, chervil or tarragon | | |
| a pinch of salt | | |
| 1 chopped shallot or onion | | |
| 200 ml | 7 fl oz | poultry, veal or fish stock |
| 200 ml | 7 fl oz | cream |
| 2 tbs freshly chopped chervil, tarragon or chives (for garnish) | | |
| salt, pepper | | |
| a pinch of cayenne pepper | | |

Mix together the white wine, chopped chives, chervil or tarragon, a pinch of salt, chopped onion and stock, as required, and reduce to 100 ml/4 fl oz of liquid. Strain through a sieve and stir in the cream over gentle heat. Allow the sauce to thicken and just before serving add garnish of the chopped chives, chervil or tarragon and season the sauce.

This sauce goes well with veal, poultry or fish dishes.

## Morel or mushroom sauce

| | | |
|---|---|---|
| 30 g | 1 oz | dried morels or |
| 300 g | 10 oz | fresh mushrooms |
| 1 finely chopped onion | | |
| 2 tbs butter | | |
| 100 ml | 4 fl oz | dry white wine |
| 1 tbs much-reduced veal or poultry stock (optional) | | |
| 250 ml | 8 fl oz | single or double cream |
| salt, freshly ground pepper | | |
| a pinch of cayenne pepper | | |
| 2 drops of lemon juice | | |

Soak the dried morels in warm water until soft enough to use, then cut them in half lengthwise and wash well. Strain the water which was used to soak them through a coffee filter. Clean the fresh mushrooms and slice.

Sweat the cleaned morels or mushroom slices with the chopped onion in butter. Add the white wine, reduced stock and the water the morels were soaked in and reduce quickly. Add the cream and cook until a creamy sauce is obtained. Season with salt, pepper, cayenne pepper and lemon juice. This sauce goes well with veal, sweetbreads or poultry.

# Marrow sauce

| | | |
|---|---|---|
| 1 chopped shallot or onion | | |
| 1 tbs butter | | |
| 3 crushed peppercorns | | |
| 1 small sprig of thyme | | |
| 1 small bay leaf | | |
| 100 ml | 4 fl oz | dry white or red wine |
| 300 ml | 12 fl oz | brown veal broth |
| salt, pepper | | |
| 3 marrow bones (approx 120 g/4 oz beef marrow) | | |
| 1 tbs butter | | |

Sweat the chopped shallot in the butter. Add the pepper-corns, thyme, bay leaf and wine and reduce until about 3 tablespoons of liquid remain. Add the veal stock, reduce again, pass the sauce through a sieve and season. Cut the marrow into small dice or slices and blanch in salt water. Add the blanched cubes of marrow to the sauce and finish it with a tablespoon of butter.

*Tip:* Place the marrow bones in cold water for an hour; this way the marrow is more easily removed.

# Game sauce

| | | |
|---|---|---|
| 100 ml | 4 fl oz | red Burgandy |
| meat juices | | |
| 200–300 ml | $\frac{1}{3}$–$\frac{1}{2}$ pint | game stock |
| 1 tbs cranberry or redcurrant jelly | | |
| salt, freshly ground pepper | | |
| a pinch of cayenne pepper | | |
| 1 tbs cognac | | |
| cream or butter for binding | | |

Mix the red wine with the meat juices (after browning the meat). Add the game stock and reduce a little. Add the cranberry or redcurrant jelly, salt, pepper, a pinch of cayenne pepper and the cognac.

Strain the sauce and bind with a little cream or butter.

## General notes

**Ingredients.** A perfect sauce demands the best ingredients: good butter, fresh eggs, carefully made stock.

**Straining.** Straining the finished sauce gives an elegant smoothness. Professional chefs pour the sauce into a muslin cloth (*tamis*) and two chefs, one at each end, twist the cloth to squeeze out the sauce.

**Reducing.** To reduce a sauce, lower the heat and simmer very slowly until the liquid evaporates and is reduced by as much as half, or even more. Stir brown sauces just often enough to keep them from sticking to the pan and burning. White sauces improve in colour and texture the more they are whipped. During this long, slow process the flavours of the ingredients are extracted and blended and the starch thoroughly cooked so that the sauce has a velvety texture, obtainable in no other way.

**Consistency.** A sauce of correct consistency will, when stirred, coat the back of a spoon.

**To remove fat from a sauce,** greatly reduce the heat and throw a few drops of cold water into the pan. This at once causes the fat to rise to the surface and then it can easily be removed with a spoon.

# Roasts

## RICHARD OLNEY

In the past a clean distinction existed between the terms baking and roasting. Baking meant oven cookery; a roast was any beast or joint that revolved on a turnspit before an open fire. Today most roasts are baked but, to our ultimate confusion, the same distinction in terminology has been retained; any meat that, because of its shape, is susceptible of being spitted is called a roast whereas a flat object – a bird that has been split down the back and flattened or a split and opened-out sheep's head, for instance – is said to be baked.

### OPEN-FIRE ROASTING

Many cooks are convinced of the superiority of open-fire roasting although, unlike meats that are grilled over wood embers, a roast that revolves before a fireplace, receiving heat by horizontal rather than by vertical convection, acquires little flavour from the wood. But the case for open-fire roasting need not be pleaded; the sheer beauty of the thing is sufficient justification. The intimacy of the cook's involvement, bringing all the senses into play as the slow-turning roast progressively alters, suddenly begins to assume a golden colour, demands to be basted, first with its own fat or with a bit of olive oil or butter and later, with certain meats, as their juices begin to break through the surface, with an occasional splash of wine or other liquid thrown first into the dripping pan until, finally, the pale gold deepens to a caramel glaze, is unlike any other cooking experience.

Rapid roasts – small game birds, for instance – should be turned at close proximity to an intense wall of flames. A large joint, after an initial searing, should cook before a more regular fire, but one of greater depth fed by larger logs, the heat emanating more from the embers than from an abundance of flame. The heat may be controlled by deliberately permitting the fire to die down, by raising or lowering the spit by a notch or two or, if it is a portable turnspit, by moving it closer to or farther from the fire. The motion of the turnspit may be momentarily arrested toward the end of the cooking if one side of a joint requires more colour or cooking than another. Fireplace roasting requires slightly more time than oven roasting – as little as a couple of minutes more for snipe or quail, about 5 minutes longer for a pheasant or a $1\frac{1}{2}$ kg/3 lb chicken, some 10 minutes longer for a leg of lamb and as much as half an hour more for a stuffed suckling pig . . . but this is abstract theory, based on the unreal premise of all things being equal; in fact, one must sense the moment that a roast is ready. No doubt, open-fire roasting encourages the cultivation of a certain intuition that is too rarely applied to oven cookery.

Gas or electrical rotisseries with a heat source either above or behind the turnspit and a dripping pan beneath operate on the same principle as open-fire roasting. Barbecues are sometimes fitted with a turnspit that revolves over incandescent charcoal. The result can be very good if the charcoal has not been chemically treated but, because the juices are lost in the coals, this method is best adapted to roasts that demand no more than 40 to 45 minutes' cooking.

## OVEN ROASTING

The initial rule in oven roasting is to know your oven. The cooker should be absolutely level to avoid fats and juices burning in the roasting pan. Professional ovens heat more regularly than most home ovens and for this reason can be used at higher temperatures for high-heat roasting or searing. But no oven heats with perfect regularity from all sides. Your oven's particular bad habits will dictate how and how often the position of a roasting pan or a roast should be shifted. Some ovens are more hermetic than others. A good oven that holds its heat for a long period of time will allow you to cook a leg of lamb at searing temperature for ten minutes before turning the oven off and leaving the roast to its own devices for an hour or so. It will continue to cook at a progressively lowering temperature and its resting period will be incorporated into the total length of time spent in the oven.

Mechanical devices may be useful for general indications, but depending blindly upon them can only produce mechanical, impersonal and imperfect food.

1. Thermostats often do not register correctly and, in any case, the cook should feel free to turn the heat up or down, several times if necessary, depending on the progression – the look or the feel – of the roast. (A professional cook pinches, pokes, smells, looks, listens, shifts from hot ovens to slow ovens, holds a roast on top of the stove, then tucks it into a warming oven . . . and so forth.)

2. Meat thermometers can never indicate precisely when a roast should be removed from the oven if only because a resting period in a warm place, during which the internal temperature of the roast continues to rise, is useful for most roasts and essential, in particular, to those that are kept rare or pink.

3. Timing charts or suggestions are meant to guide the cook in the right direction but, if respected absolutely, will rarely give perfect results, for there are too many particulars to be taken into account: a) A roasting pan with low sides will permit a more rapid and even colouration than one with relatively high sides that frustrate the even distribution of heat. (High sides may, however, present a

distinct advantage for a large joint like a beef rib roast which must not colour too rapidly because of its prolonged stay in the oven.) b) Any roasting pan should be of heavy material, but a roast will cook more quickly in a black iron pan than in a tinned copper roasting pan, an aluminium pan or a light-coloured enamelled iron pan because black absorbs heat more readily, whereas light colours tend to repel it (black pans, therefore, may be advantageous for small roasts but not so for a large joint). c) Meats that are relatively fresh take longer to cook than aged meats or hung game. (A dozen partridges of the same size and all young, neatly spaced in a large roasting pan and roasted together in a hot oven for the requisite 18 minutes, even though the pan and the birds may be shuffled around during roasting to equalise the heat, will never present exactly the same degree of doneness. Some may be perfectly cooked, others slightly underdone and the breasts of others may no longer hold a pink cast when cut into.) d) The thickness of a roast is more important in judging its cooking time than the weight. A 2–2½ kg/4–5 lb section of *contre filet* and a 4 kg/8 lb section of the same cut will be cooked in approximately the same length of time. A compactly shaped joint will require a longer cooking period per unit of weight than an elongated or flatter shape, and an unboned joint will take longer than a boneless roast of the same weight and quality. e) Even amongst relatively tender cuts, those muscles that receive more exercise will require a somewhat longer cooking period. f) The larger the roast, the shorter the cooking time per unit of weight and, after an initial searing, the lower the temperature. A small roast is cooked at a higher temperature than a large roast from the same cut. g) No matter what the thermostat registers, when a roast is put into the oven the temperature goes down. The smaller the oven, the larger the roast or, in the case of birds, the greater the number, the more drastic the loss of heat – and, in the latter case, the more irregular the circulation of heat.

It is often said that roasts must be placed on grills and

never touch the bottom of the pan lest they contract a stewed taste and that one must never salt a roast until it is half-cooked for fear of drawing out valuable juices. I am unconvinced and, in fact, with high-heat roasting, it seems not only of the greatest importance that the roast rest directly on the bottom of the pan but that the pan itself be of a size just to contain the roast to avoid fat burning in unprotected spaces. A choice of heavy frying pans and gratin dishes is useful for fitting a pan to a roast.

It is also said that a roast must be basted only with fat and never with a liquid, but such a purist definition condemns an entire category of sumptuous preparations that, although technically the beginning of a braising process may have set in, cannot sensibly be called by another name than roast. These are roasts (usually of veal, pork or other meats that are traditionally served well done but, with care, a leg of lamb may be treated in this way also and still remain pink) to which, after most of the fat has been removed from the pan toward the end of the cooking period, a small amount of liquid is added – often repeatedly since there must never be more than a few spoonsful in the pan at a time – and the meat is then basted over and over again at very short intervals until a rich glaze is formed on the surface. The liquid is often white wine, sometimes a fortified wine, or it may be the reserved marinade. Or, with veal or hutch rabbit, for instance, as the first addition of deglazing liquid disappears, it may be replaced by double (heavy) cream or a film of prepared mustard and then cream spread over and the roast returned to the oven for continued basting until it is coated in a thick, caramel-coloured sauce.

## STUFFINGS

Stuffings are pretty much interchangeable from one meat to another although sage and onion stuffing should probably be restricted to poultry and suckling pig. Meats that are best rare or pink do not easily lend themselves to being stuffed. Home-made sausage meat (2 parts of lean to 1 of fat), semi-fresh breadcrumbs, or fresh curd cheese are good bases with which to work, alone or in combination. Parboiled rice can replace the breadcrumbs, rapidly parboiled, refreshed, squeezed and chopped chard or spinach can be a wonderful addition as, of course, can the liver, heart and trimmed gizzard lobes of the bird, cut small and rapidly sautéed to firm them, or the chopped trimmings from the meat. These stuffings are usually bound with eggs and, if no other fat is present, some soft butter can be worked in. Chopped, butter-stewed onion or shallot, *duxelles* or chopped and sautéed wild mushrooms, chopped truffle peelings or fragments, garlic pounded to a paste with a bit of coarse salt and mixed with chopped parsley, mixed herbs and spices,* wine and brandy are good aromatic supports; in short, choose what you like, add what you like, season to taste and mix well, using your hands.

## PARTICULARITIES AND TIMING

Roasts should be at room temperature when put to cook. Stuffings should be considered as part of the total weight

---

* A good herb mixture for general use consists of thyme, oregano, marjoram and winter savory in descending proportions. The first three are best picked at the moment of flowering. All are dried in bundles and later assembled, first crumbled off the stems, semi-pulverised in a food processor and then sieved to remove fragments of branches before being stored away. Except for oregano, which is always better dried, they may also be used fresh; the tender spring shoots of winter savory and the budding, unopened flowers of marjoram are particularly attractive. Rosemary and sage, both of which are violent herbs and require circumspection, are better fresh. The usual spices are nutmeg, mace, allspice, cayenne, and pepper, all of which are best pounded, ground or grated at the moment of use although professional cooks often make up herb and spice mixtures for general use.

when timing a roast. Your oven and your experience must dictate the degree to which the following timings are respected. For most of the larger joints I have suggested a 10 minute searing at gas 8/230°C/450°F, followed by a reduction in temperature, sometimes progressive and always proportionately lower the larger the roast, followed by a resting period in a warm place, the length of which is proportionately longer the larger the roast. Equally good results may be had, with a good oven, by heating it to its highest setting, gas 10–12/260–290°C/500–550°F, and reducing the heat as soon as you have closed the oven door. One way or another, it is possible to count somewhat more roasting time per unit of weight at relatively lower temperatures.

It should be remembered that the resting period is, in fact, a radically slowed down continuation of the cooking process as the heat, superficially absorbed from a hot oven, penetrates to the heart of the roast, the interior temperature continuing to rise. It is, at the same time, a tenderising process. A 3 kg/6 lb leg of lamb, for example, that has spent 50 minutes to an hour in the oven will, if carved immediately, pour out an abundance of juices, the centre will be very rare and the texture somewhat rubbery; if left to relax in a warm place for 20 minutes or so, the meat will be pink instead of bloody, the juices, having been reintegrated into the flesh, will not flow out as it is sliced and the rubbery resistance beneath the tooth will have given way to melting tenderness. In the home kitchen, the choice of a warm place is usually a turned-off oven that has been permitted to cool somewhat; if the kitchen's only oven remains in use, the roast will have to be held at the back of the stove. Because roasts are never as hot as braised meats which are penetrated by heat to a saturation point and because of the loss of heat during the resting period, it is especially important that these roasts be served on hot plates.

The estimated timings are for rare beef, pink lamb and game and well done pork, veal and poultry. Preferences may vary concerning degrees of rareness, but those meats that are always served well done should, nonetheless, remain moist. Over-roasted meat is dry and savourless. With only two exceptions that I can think of, *no meat requires more than 20 minutes per 500 g/1 lb*. The exceptions are the roasts, described above, that are subjected to the beginning of a braising process through a final period of basting with a liquid to form a glaze, and firm cuts, usually of beef, whose virtues lie more in price and flavour than in tenderness, that are cooked without searing at a very low temperature throughout – for a 3 kg/6 or 7 lb silverside or 'leg-of-mutton' cut, about 25 minutes per 500 g/1 lb at gas 1/140°C/275°F.

For traditional roasts that are basted only with fat, the gravy is prepared after the roast is removed from the pan; most of the fat is spooned off and the pan is deglazed over heat by the addition of a liquid while the solidified meat juices adhering to the bottom and the sides of the pan are scraped with a wooden spoon to loosen them and permit them to dissolve in the boiling liquid, which is then reduced to a few spoonsful. The choice of liquid is a matter of taste. Many cooks conscientiously use water for beef so as not to denature the flavour. Personally, I prefer white wine for most meats. Brandy is sometimes used, in part, for game birds but, for many tastes, may be best restricted to woodcock. Very little gravy can be prepared from rare roasts and many people prefer the unadulterated carving juices which, if not served as such, should, as soon as the roast is carved, be added to the gravy-boat before it is passed.

## Beef

Because of the size of the animal, most cuts of beef are boned out, respecting the basic muscular structure. The exception is a rib roast which loses greatly in succulence through boning; to facilitate carving, the chine bone should be sawn through at the point where it joins the ribs before roasting so that, at table, it may be neatly sliced off and set aside. Cuts that are not protected by a natural layer of fat are usually barded, preferably with beef fat. A fillet is trimmed of superficial fat and membranes and the *filet mignon*\* is folded double and tied to equalise the roast's thickness. Barding is unnecessary for a rare fillet because of its unusually short cooking time. It need only be smeared with butter or oil. The characteristic clean and robust flavour of beef is not improved by the association with herbs, marinades or other aromatics. The flavour is heightened and the flesh tenderised by discreet ageing – your butcher's affair.

**Rib roast:** 8 to 10 minutes per 500 g/1 lb. Gas 8/230°C/450°F for the first 10 minutes with progressive reduction, first to gas 4/180°C/350°F, then gas 3–2/160–150°C/325–300°F. At least a 30 minute rest in a warm place.

**Fillet:** 4 to 7 minutes per 500 g/1 lb. Gas 8/230°C/450°F for the first 10 minutes, remainder at gas 3/160°C/325°F. 15 minute rest.

**Contre-filet:** Same as fillet.

**Rump roast:** 8 to 10 minutes per 500 g/1 lb. Gas 8/230°C/450°F for the first 10 minutes, remainder at gas 4/180°C/350°F. 15 minute rest.

## Veal

Veal roasts are nearly always boned out, the rib section being sold as chops. Roasts are usually barded with sheets of pork back fat – a criss-cross pattern of strips instead of the usual solid sheet will permit the meat to take on good

---

\* The *filet mignon*, in beef, is the narrow tip of the fillet or tenderloin; in other animals the entire tenderloin is known as the *filet mignon* and the loin becomes the *filet*. Loin of beef, in French, is called either *contre-filet* or *faux-filet* but, in England, it is often called *entrecôte* (which, in French, is the boned-out rib section). The *filet* and the *filet mignon* in birds are the large and the small muscles of each half breast.

colour while being nourished with the fat at the same time. Wrapping in pork caul gives equally good and attractive results (caul is usually sold salted in England and should first be soaked briefly, rinsed and laid out on a towel to dry). Sprigs of fresh sage or rosemary are often tied up with a veal roast. Veal produces much the greatest abundance of juice of any roast and is particularly admired for its gravy; should any be left over, it is an invaluable addition to any number of braised dishes or sauces. A roast calf's liver is one of the great delicacies. The thin membrane that covers the liver should be removed and the liver rubbed with olive oil, seasoned with salt just before being put to roast. It is not necessary that it be a whole liver but it should be at least 1 kg/2 lb in a compact shape.

**Veal roasts:** 15 minutes per 500 g/1 lb for large roasts. 18 to 20 minutes per 500 g/1 lb for smaller roasts, at gas 4/180°C/350°F. 15 minute rest.

**Calf's liver:** 10 minutes per 500 g/1 lb. Gas 8/230°C/450°F for the first 10 minutes, reduce the heat progressively to gas 2/150°C/300°F. 10 to 15 minute rest.

## Pork

The section of pelvic bone remaining in a leg of pork should be removed for ease in carving. A loin is often boned and stuffed before being rolled and tied. The two racks of ribs may be chined and trimmed to form a crown that is stuffed. The complicated section known as the neck end, containing a section of the shoulder blade and the spare rib, is usually boned out and often stuffed. The skin is removed from most pork roasts (this is essential if the roast is to be glazed) and the fat trimmed to an even thickness. Both the flavour and the digestibility of fresh pork are improved if, after boning, it is salted down overnight with a handful of coarse salt and a good pinch of mixed herbs. The liquid that is drawn out is discarded and the meat rubbed free of any clinging salt (and, of course, no salt is added during cooking), or it may be rapidly rinsed and sponged dry. Fresh sage or rosemary, garlic, truffles or fruits are often associated with pork. A boned loin lends itself, by its form, to being stuffed with a row of truffle pieces or with dried apricots or pitted prunes, first macerated for an hour or so in white wine. If truffles are used, it is best to prepare the roast a day ahead of time to permit the bouquet to penetrate the flesh. Suckling pig or a leg on which the skin has been left for crackling must be scored to prevent the skin's buckling and, for crisp crackling, the skin should be rubbed with olive oil before going into the oven and basted throughout the cooking only with fat, avoiding any juices in the bottom of the pan that may have been drawn out of the meat.

**Leg (whole):** 18 minutes per 500 g/1 lb. Gas 8/230°C/450°F for first 10 minutes, reducing progressively to gas 4/180°C/350°F, and finally to gas 3/160°C/325°F. 30 minute rest.

**Other cuts (including half legs, either knuckle end or fillet end):** 20 minutes per 500 g/1 lb. Gas 8/230°C/450°F for first 10 minutes, gas 4/180°C/350°F for remainder. 15 minute rest.

**Whole stuffed suckling pig:** 10 to 12 minutes per 500 g/1 lb. Gas 4/180°C/350°F, reducing to gas 3/160°C/325°F if necessary to slow down colouration. 30 minute rest.

## Lamb and mutton

Milk lamb and baby goat are rarely available. Baby goats weigh from 4 to 5 kg/8 to 10 lb when cleaned and milk lambs up to 6 kg/12 lb. Although sometimes halved or quartered, they are usually roasted whole, first wrapped in their caul or, lacking that, in pig's caul, and should be well done. They are improved by being marinated with a mixture of herbs and a little olive oil before being roasted and should be basted only with their fat so as to form a crisp golden surface.

The animals marketed as lamb vary from three or four months to a year of age, depending on the time of year. For all practical purposes, they are young mutton and should be treated as mature animals. The colour of the flesh may vary from rose-beige to a deep, clear amaranth depending on the animal's age. To remain succulent, it should be kept quite pink. For the sake of neat carving, the section of pelvic bone must be removed from the leg joint and the tip end of the knuckle sawn off (ask your butcher not to cut or saw through the middle of the roast). The handle device known as a *manche à gigot* that screws or clamps on to the bone end of a leg of lamb or venison will lend elegance and ease to carving.

A saddle always suffers from boning. For correct carving, none of the haunch or pelvic bone should be included in the cut, but one or two floating ribs are usually included and boned out and a section of apron is left to each side that is rolled beneath the roast to protect the *filets mignons* during cooking. To carve, cut straight down the length of the saddle, following the contour of the spinal bones to partially free the loin or *filet*, then cut in toward the bone structure horizontally to remove slices the length of the saddle. Slice the other *filet* in the same way, turn the joint over, remove the aprons and the *filets mignons* in their entire length and slice each across into sections.

A rack is usually chined so that the roast may be carved between the ribs to fall into chops. Because the complicated bone structure of a shoulder does not permit of neat carving, it is usually boned and rolled (although the meat is better if unboned).

To avoid the flavour, sometimes described as woolly, which resides not in the delicate flesh but in the fat, remove nearly all the fat from any lamb or mutton roast (in any case, the skin must be removed from a saddle or a rack) and rub it with olive oil and mixed herbs. In Italy, rosemary is often allied with lamb and, in Greece, oregano. The habit of tucking spikes of garlic into slits in a leg of lamb results only in one's guests biting into chunks of raw garlic. To flavour the inside of a leg, better results will be had by pounding garlic to a paste with some coarse salt and adding mixed herbs, freshly ground pepper and a little white wine to loosen the mixture; then, on the bias, pierce deep slits with the tip of a sharp knife, forcing each open with your finger, and spoon some of the mixture into each, rubbing the remainder all over the surface of the meat. A leg prepared in this way can also profit by marinating in a supplementary dash of white wine and a spoonful or so of olive oil, and it should be well drained and rubbed in olive oil before being roasted. The marinade is used either for regular basting after the first 45 minutes or for deglazing the roasting pan after removing the leg. Another way to flavour a roast with garlic is to throw a handful of unpeeled garlic cloves into the roasting pan to flavour the basting juices. Alternatively, 20 or 30 firm, fresh garlic cloves may be peeled, parboiled in salted water for 12–15 minutes or until tender but firmly intact, drained and simmered for a few minutes in a small saucepan with the deglazed roasting juices. To these are added the carving juices before being served over the slices of meat.

**Leg:** 9 to 10 minutes per 500 g/1 lb. Gas 8/230°C/450°F for the first 10 minutes, progressive reduction to gas 3/160°C/325°F. 15 to 30 minute rest.

**Baron (2 legs and part or all of the saddle in a single piece):** About 6 to 7 minutes per 500 g/1 lb. Gas 8/230°C/450°F for the first 10 minutes, progressive reduction to gas 2/150°C/300°F. At least a 30 minute rest.

**Saddle:** 6 to 8 minutes per 500 g/1 lb. First 10 minutes at gas 8/230°C/450°F, remainder at gas 4/175°C/350°F. 15 minute rest.

**Rack:** 15 minutes at gas 8/230°C/450°F. 10 minute rest. (If tied into a guards-of-honour roast, treat like a saddle.)

**Shoulder (boned and rolled):** 10 minutes per 500 g/1 lb. Gas 8/230°C/450°F for the first 10 minutes, progressive reduction to gas 3/160°C/325°F. 15 minute rest. (If unboned, roast for 30–35 minutes, same temperatures and resting time.)

**Whole milk lamb or baby goat:** 10 minutes per 500 g/1 lb. Gas 8/230°C/450°F for the first 10 minutes, progressive reduction to gas 3/160°C/325°F. 15 minute rest.

## Venison

A leg of venison is called a haunch. The pelvic bone should be removed and the knuckle end of the bone sawn off as for a leg of lamb and a *manche à gigot* will facilitate carving. Because the flesh is so lean, the entire visible surface is often larded. A hinged larding needle is most practical. The lardons are cut from chilled pork back fat, first sliced barely $\frac{1}{2}$ cm/$\frac{1}{4}$ inch thick, each slice cut into strips of the same width. With the needle they are drawn into and out of the flesh in deep stitches at approximately 2 cm/$\frac{3}{4}$ inch intervals, each stitch about $2\frac{1}{2}$ cm/1 inch in length, and in alternating rows, the needle piercing and leaving the flesh on a line with and at an intermediate point between the incisions of the preceding row and the row to follow. The lardons are trimmed to leave about 1 cm/$\frac{1}{2}$ inch visible at each end.

Often the entire back of venison, from haunch to neck, with the ribs cut short, is sold as saddle. It is more practical to cut venison in the same way as lamb, using the rack as a separate roast or cutting it into chops for grilling. A tough membrane covers the flesh of a saddle and can be removed with a sharp, flexible knife in sheet-like sections, cutting it first free from the ridge of the backbone and pulling at the loosened extremity of membrane with one hand while shaving it free with the knife blade held flatly at a very slight bias upward so as not to cut into the flesh. A saddle is often barded or larded but, because it requires a relatively short cooking time, an envelope of caul will nourish it sufficiently and the lace will melt into a lovely brown surface that forms an integral part of the roast. The caul-wrapped roast should be smeared with olive oil.

Because of the complication of nervous tissue in a venison shoulder, it is more suitable as a braising cut.

Venison is often marinated – sometimes for two or three days – before roasting, either in a raw marinade (wine, a bit of vinegar, oil, aromatic vegetables, herbs and spices) or in a cooked marinade (same elements with a higher proportion of vinegar, boiled for half an hour and cooled before using). This will tenderise tough flesh but, if the animal is young, the flesh is tender and immersion in an acidic marinade will destroy the delicacy of flavour. (A few hours with a pinch of mixed herbs and a dash each of olive oil and white wine will do no harm.) Hanging in a cold, dry atmosphere or in a cold room for several days or a week before being cut up will tenderise the flesh and improve the flavour.

Venison roasts are usually accompanied by a game sauce. In the home kitchen it can be useful to freeze scraps, trimmings, heads and necks of wild rabbits and hare, scraps of venison, necks and left-over carcasses of roast game birds, grouse legs and so forth in order to gather together at a given time as much material as possible from which to draw flavour. Spread as many scraps, trimmings and carcasses, roughly chopped up, as possible into a large roasting pan with coarsely chopped onions and carrots, parsley stems and roots (if possible, or throw in a chopped parsnip), branches of thyme, a stick of celery, a bay leaf and a few juniper berries. Dribble with olive oil and toss around so that all of the elements are more or less coated with a film of oil and put the pan into a hot oven for a good half hour, giving the contents a stir from time to time to prevent them from sticking and to give all the surfaces a good colour. Scatter a small handful of flour over, stir well and return the pan to the oven until the flour browns lightly, then add a healthy dash of vinegar and about half a bottle of white wine, stir and scrape the bottom and sides of the pan to dissolve caramelised adherences and return to the oven until the liquid is reduced to no more than enough to coat the meats and vegetables. Transfer everything to a large saucepan, wash out the roasting pan with more white wine and add it, along with about 1 litre/1½ pints of rich veal stock, to the saucepan, bring to the boil, and simmer with the lid slightly ajar for three or four hours or more. Transfer to a large sieve, collecting the sauce in a bowl beneath and pressing the contents of the sieve firmly with a pestle to extract all juices. Pour the sauce into another saucepan (as nearly as possible one that just contains it for ease in skimming), bring to the boil and set the saucepan half off a low heat to maintain a very light boil to one side of the surface only, permitting a skin containing fat and other impurities to form on the still side of the surface. The longer you wait, the easier it will be to remove the skin without skimming out and discarding valuable sauce. Each time a firm and manageable skin is formed, gently gather it to the edge of the saucepan with a spoon, lift it out and discard it until, after an hour or so, the skin that forms is no more than a transparent veil displaying tiny wrinkles, no longer containing any trace of fat or other foreign substance. You should now have about a half litre/a pint or somewhat less of intensely flavoured but light-bodied sauce of a deep but semi-translucent mahogany cast. If 8 or 10 bruised peppercorns are thrown in a few minutes before removing it from the heat and straining it through a fine sieve into a heated sauce-boat, it is called a *poivrade* sauce. Cream may be added to it before it is sieved – no more than 100 ml/3–4 fl oz for this quantity of sauce and, if one likes, a spoonful of redcurrant jelly may first be melted in a *bain-marie* or over low heat and stirred into the cream before it is added.

Deglazing juices from the roast are often added to a sauce but this troubles its clarity and hardly alters its flavour – best save them, if a sauce is served, for use with leftovers.

**Roast venison:** Same temperatures, cooking and resting time as for lamb, remembering that many people like venison rarer than lamb. It is of the greatest importance that it not be overcooked – a few minutes too many in the oven will transform a succulent cut of venison into irremediably dry and tasteless stuff, whereas a few minutes too few for a perfect degree of pinkness will simply produce delicious rare meat. Use your judgement.

## Hare and rabbit

Hare and wild rabbit should be young (the fragility of the ears, which are easily torn, is the easiest indication of youth) and hung for no more than a day or so – long enough to permit the flesh to relax. They are often marinated but this, like prolonged hanging, alters the flesh, destroying the clean, natural savour. Either, like venison, may be accompanied by a game sauce. This is most often done with hare. When the animal has been skinned and gutted, the liver hangs free in the abdominal cavity at its attachment to the diaphragm. It should be carefully detached and the gall bladder cut out and discarded. Behind the diaphragm, in the chest cavity which contains the heart and the lungs, the blood collects and, after the diaphragm is slit open, it is usually poured into a bowl, stirred with a little vinegar to prevent coagulation and saved, either to prepare a *civet* with the parts of a hare not used for roasting or to transform a *poivrade* sauce into a *civet* sauce to accompany the roast saddle of hare. The liver and lungs are often puréed into the blood before incorporating it into the sauce (a whir in a processor before passing everything through a sieve is the most practical method). The same care should be taken as with an egg-yolk-thickened sauce, a ladle of warm sauce being first stirred into the blood before the lot is stirred back into the slightly cooled sauce and returned to low heat, stirring the while, until the sauce turns the colour of dark bitter chocolate and thickens to a smooth velvet. If it is permitted to boil it will break into a fine, granular suspension.

Because the legs take longer to cook and much of the finesse is lost if the saddle is not kept quite rare, it is common practice to roast only a saddle of hare, reserving the rest for a *civet* or a terrine. To include the entire length of the *filet*, it is cut from the haunch to the neck with the ribs trimmed short. Because the cooking time is so brief it need neither be larded nor wrapped in caul – a generous smear of butter or olive oil will do – and, to avoid masking its firm flavour, seasoning is best confined to salt and pepper. As with venison, a tough membrane clings to the tender flesh of a saddle of hare. Professional cooks remove it, but it is less troublesome than that of venison and difficult to remove without damaging the flesh – you may prefer to leave it. A single saddle can only serve two. It is carved by removing the *filets* from the spinal structure and slicing them thinly on the bias then turning the roast over to remove the *filets mignons* which are served whole.

Because wild rabbit is so small, it is roasted whole, the elbow joints of the forelegs dislocated so that they may be drawn backward to lie straight against the body, fixed by a length of string drawn by a trussing needle through the shoulders and the body, back through the lower joints of the forelegs and the body, and tied; the shank bones of the hind legs are crossed and tied. The head may be left or removed depending on personal sensibilities. An envelope of caul and a dribble of olive oil will protect and nourish the flesh; salt, a few turns of the pepper mill and a sprinkle of mixed herbs will season it nicely. It is carved as if being cut up for a stew, the hind legs removed by cutting across the body and split to one side or the other of the tail to separate them, the saddle cut crosswise into two sections and the ribcage split lengthwise leaving a foreleg attached to each half.

Hutch rabbits are sacrificed for the market at a tender four months. They should be cooked until well done. The flavour is bland and a few hours in a marinade of white wine, herbs, a sliced onion, a couple of bruised garlic cloves and a dash of olive oil will lend a spark to it. A hutch rabbit may then be prepared like a wild rabbit or it may be cut in two at the beginning of the ribcage, the floating ribs and the spinal column boned out of the saddle, the hind legs left intact, and the flesh scraped from the upper part of the body incorporated into a stuffing. The back and hind legs may be larded as for haunch of venison.

**Saddle of hare:** 10 minutes at gas 9/260°C/500°F. 5 minutes with oven turned off.

**Wild rabbit (usually 750 g–1 kg/1½–2 pounds):** about 25 minutes in all. Gas 8/230°C/450°F for the first 10 minutes, gas 4/180°C/350°F for the remainder. 10 minute rest.

**Hutch rabbit (usually 1½–2 kg/3–4 pounds):** 15 minutes per 500 g/1 kg. Gas 8/230°C/450°F for the first 10 minutes, gas 4/180°C/350°F for the remainder. 10 minute rest.

## Poultry and game birds

The days are past when a woodcock was hung first by a foot until droplets of green fluid oozed from the beak and was then hung by the head until the body dropped off before being plucked and roasted. In France certain hunters have a particular affection for partridge that is prepared and roasted the moment it is shot – *au bout du fusil* – well before rigor mortis sets in. These extremes aside, it is safe to say that most game birds need to hang in the feather (they are always best plucked just before cooking) for a certain time during which the flesh becomes more tender and the flavour is heightened. This is more important for some birds than for others and the ideal time may vary from a day or two to a week. A pheasant, for instance, is always dry and tasteless if too fresh whereas, hung for five days to a week, the flesh roasted to a delicate pink, it is amongst the most subtle and succulent of meats. Woodcock requires about the same length of hanging for its characteristic flavour to develop. Snipe can do with a couple of days less. Wild quail (those on the market are all farmed these days) and wild duck should be quite fresh – a day or so for the quail and no more than two or three for the duck – and both grouse and partridge are at their best with three to four days' hanging. The time of year may also indicate a more or less long period of hanging; unless the birds are hung in a refrigerated cold room, they should hang for a shorter time during relatively warm weather, whereas a day or two longer at the height of winter will do no harm. Any bird, however, that has received shot in the abdomen is best plucked and cleaned immediately to avoid intestinal putrefaction; it may be refrigerated for a couple of days, unwrapped and placed on a grill to permit a free circulation of air.

For tender roasts all birds should be young. Supple beaks (or bills) and breastbones, a pointed rather than rounded tip to the longest wing feather, delicate, thinly scaled feet rather than feet heavily encrusted with coarse scales are all indications of youth.

The breast of any bird large enough to carve can be cut into neat slices all the way to the breastbone if the wishbone is removed before trussing. If the neckskin is pulled back to bare the upper part of the breast, the position of the wishbone can easily be seen. With the tip of a small knife, slit the flesh, following the contour of the wishbone, severing, at the same time, its attachment to the tip of the breastbone; when it is completely detached from the flesh, slip a finger into the inverted V-shape and pull it backward, freeing it from the shoulder joints.

For aesthetic reasons the oil ducts, which lie above the tail, are removed from larger birds. This is particularly important with ducks for, with certain varieties, these ducts can taint the flesh with what is described as a musky odour or taste.

Today's prices forbid the ancient practice of stuffing chickens or turkeys with truffles but, by gently loosening the skin from the flesh of the breast and the legs, a single truffle, thinly sliced and distributed between skin and flesh, can impart a surprising intensity of flavour, particularly if the truffle is fresh and the bird prepared a day in advance. Snail butter or various other herb butters, *duxelles* or *mirepoix* can be administered in the same way.

If not stuffed, seasoning and a chunk of butter can be tucked into the body cavity of a chicken or turkey before trussing. Some cooks prefer to replace the butter with cream cheese or fresh curd cheese. A branch of thyme, a bouquet of tarragon or a small sprig of rosemary will delicately perfume the flesh. Bread or rice-based stuffings are usual. A turkey, because of its unusually deep throat cavity, the strong clavicles and the small opening from the throat to the body cavity, is often stuffed with two different mixtures, a sausage-based stuffing reserved for the throat. Apples may be put into a goose to flavour the flesh; they are not served. Game birds are sometimes stuffed (at times rather grandly with *foie gras* and truffles), but a stuffing imposes extra cooking and inevitably overcooked breasts.

Large birds are most neatly trussed with two lengths of string: the first with the needle run through the wings near the shoulder joint and through the back, at the same time pinning the folded-back flap of neckskin into place on the back and, after first folding the legs into place high up to the sides of the breast, back through the thighs and the body near the drumstick joint, the string ends tied tightly; the second through the lower end of the wings and the body and back through the lower end of the drumsticks, beneath the bones, and through the lower part of the carcass, pinning the drumsticks tightly into place at the same time that the abdominal opening is closed. A single length of string through the middle of the wings and back, returned through the drumsticks near the thigh joint, does well enough for small game birds, poussins or pigeon squabs (tender young pigeons taken from the dovecot at the moment they are learning to fly – woodpigeons are best reserved for braising).

Woodcock and snipe are never gutted (this is true of thrush and blackbirds also in those countries where they are hunted). The intestines or 'trail' are always clean and their flavour richly enhances that of the flesh. Only the gizzard is removed to avoid the unpleasantness of biting into the gravel sack; to do so, the abominal wall is pierced to the side with the point of a small knife, the gizzard is located either by prodding with a finger or a trussing needle (it is the only small, hard lump in the intestinal mass), pierced with the trussing needle, drawn out of the vent in the abdomen and cut free from the attached bit of intestine which is tucked back inside. The long and slender-beaked snipe and the slightly larger jack-snipe are miniature versions of woodcock. They are all self-trussing. After being plucked as far as the head, the skin is torn free of the neck and peeled from the head (taking the eyes with it). The heel joints of the legs are dislocated; one is folded backward at the heel and the other is folded over the bent joint with the foot tucked in between the two legs, yoga-like. The head is drawn down to the side of the body and the drumsticks and body are transpierced by the long beak near the thigh joint.

After being trussed, most game birds are barded with a sheet of fresh pork back fat held in place by a couple of rounds of string (wild ducks, although lean, have a sufficiently fatty skin to dispense with barding). Guinea fowl and pigeon squabs are also barded (in fact, both resemble game more than they do other poultry, partly, no doubt, because of their wild heritage, but also because both are sacrificed by smothering rather than by bleeding). Unlike game birds, whose bouquet is destroyed in the aggressive presence of bacon, either guinea fowl or pigeon squabs may be barded with rashers of bacon with agreeable results.

The theory that a chicken or a turkey is roasted to perfection when the leg falls free from the body ('wiggles') at the joint leads to about an hour's overcooking for a chicken and two or three hours too much for a turkey. The thickest part of the thigh of a bird, directly behind the drumstick joint, takes longest to cook. For this reason, a common test to check if poultry is well done is to pierce the thigh at this point with a trussing needle – if the juice that runs out is clear and colourless, no hint of pink remaining, the leg is well done. The problem is that when a leg is well done the breast is always overdone; for the breast to remain moist, without which all of its finesse is lost, the leg should retain a light pink blush at the joint, a quality which pleases many people and offends others. Although chicken and turkey are rarely barded, this will at least reduce the danger of the breast's drying out while, at the same time, basting the bird. Probably the only certain way to have perfectly cooked breast meat and well done legs is to detach the legs after roasting and return them to the oven or the grill.

Buttered vine leaves are often pressed to the breasts of quail or partridge before they are barded (if pheasant is treated in this way, two leaves may be necessary to cover the breast). They afford additional protection and the delicately tannic savour of the leaves leaves its trace. The fat and, if they have been used, the vine leaves, may be removed from small barded birds 4 or 5 minutes before their oven time is up to give the breasts a light golden nuance. If chickens or turkeys have been barded, the bards are removed some 15 minutes to half an hour before they come out of the oven and during this time they should be basted frequently. If not barded, chickens and turkeys should be generously smeared with butter or oil and regularly basted throughout the cooking period. For an even colouration they, as well as domestic ducks and geese, may be started on one side, turned to the other side and finished breast up (this is not useful for game birds whose short cooking time does not permit a rich colouration). A light film of oil will help ducks and geese to colour more evenly and, once the fat begins to flow, frequent basting with the hot fat will not only encourage browning but will draw out the remaining fat in the skin structure more rapidly. (Many people believe that pricking the skin repeatedly is a useful technique: if this is done, it is essential to prick very shallowly so as not to pass completely through the skin and draw out valuable juices from the flesh rather than the fat, all of which is contained in the skin itself.) Geese and ducks are usually cooked well done, the length of cooking time coinciding with the time necessary to rid the birds of excess fat. Muscovy ducks are much less fat than the Aylesbury type of duck and may be kept pink on condition that the legs be then removed and grilled for a further 10 to 15 minutes.

Because a duck's legs are so tightly wedged into the back of the body and because the breast meat of wild duck demands to be kept quite rare, the legs are still quite bloody when the breast arrives at a perfect degree of doneness. The legs of wild duck are always removed and grilled until the skin is crisp and the flesh no longer rare. The breast is carved thinly and served first and the legs are served as a separate course, accompanied by a salad.

Although grouse are roasted whole, the legs, unlike the breast which is of great delicacy, have a markedly bitter taste and are usually removed along with the lower half of the back before serving. The bitterness is attenuated by a prolonged moist cooking and they may be used for stews, game pies, stock or game sauce.

A rest in a warm place is of little importance to poultry and particularly dangerous for game birds which are inevitably overdone if held in a warm place after roasting. They should be served as rapidly as possible when removed from the oven. The exceptions are game birds which are served in a sauce made from their carcasses after roasting (pressed duck or a salmi of partridge or pheasant, for instance). The danger of overcooking in these instances is compensated by severely undercooking the birds in a blasting oven – 10 to 12 minutes for a partridge or a duck and 15 to 20 minutes for a pheasant. Woodcock is also often finished in a sauce, but its fabrication is so rapid that there is hardly any wait; the roasting pan is deglazed with brandy, the innards are scooped out and mashed with a chunk of *foie gras*, stirred into the deglazing juices, reheated briefly and a bit of butter is incorporated off the heat. For the sake of presentation, this sumptuous little dish is best arranged on individual heated plates, the sauce spread on the bottom with the split woodcock halves and the split head and beak (the brain is a particular delicacy – the beak is so constructed that the knife blade automatically follows the line of parallel ridges running above and beneath its entire length) placed on the bed of sauce, a few croûtons scattered around.

If there is enough residue to justify deglazing, a dash of white wine is as good a liquid as any with which to wash up the pan for most birds. Wild duck takes especially well to the juice of a Seville orange, supplemented by enough white wine to perform the deglazing.

Pheasants, partridges and often quail are commonly accompanied by crustless rectangles or hearts of bread, either cooked in butter until golden or toasted, spread with a *gratin* forcemeat which consists of finely chopped shallot briefly sautéed in quite a lot of butter, the birds' livers plus a chicken liver, salt and a generous turn of the pepper mill, added and sautéed only until the livers turn grey on the surface, flambéed with cognac and, when slightly cooled, either pounded in a mortar or puréed in a food processor before being passed through a fine sieve. Woodcock and snipe are presented simply on croûtons which are spread with the trail at table.

**Roast chicken:** about 15 minutes per 500 g/1 lb. The first 10 minutes at gas 8/230°C/450°F, remainder at gas 4 180°C/350°F.

**Roast turkey:** about 15 minutes per 500 g/1 lb for smaller birds and as little as 10 to 12 minutes per 500 g/ 1 lb for turkeys weighing more than 7 kg/ 15 lb. 10 minutes at gas 8/230°C/450°F, with progressive reduction to gas 3/160°C/325°F.

**Poussins and pigeon squabs:** about 25 minutes. First 10 minutes at gas 8/230°C/450°F, remainder at gas 5 190°C/375°F.

**Guinea fowl:** about 35 minutes. First 10 minutes at gas 8/230°C/450°F, remainder at gas 5/190°C/375°F.

**Goose:** about 15 minutes per 500 g/1 lb. First 10 minutes at gas 8/230°C/450°F, remainder at gas 4/180°C/350°F. The oven may be lowered more and raised toward the end of the cooking if necessary to achieve the desired colour.

**Duck:** about 20 minutes per 500 g/1 lb for 1–1½ kg/2–3 lb ducks, 15 minutes per 500 g/1 lb for larger ducks. First 10 minutes at gas 8/230°C/450°F, remainder at gas 5/190°C/375°F or lower, depending on the size of the bird.

**Wild duck:** 15 to 20 minutes at gas 8/230°C/450°F for mallard; 12 to 15 minutes at same temperature for smaller varieties such as teal.

**Quail:** 12 to 15 minutes at gas 8/230°C/450°F. (Wild quail is good pink; farmed quail should be better done, but 15 minutes will do it.)

**Grey partridge:** 18 minutes at gas 8/230°C/450°F. (Red partridge is slightly larger and can take a couple of minutes longer.)

**Grouse:** about 18 minutes at gas 8/230°C/450°F.

**Pheasant:** 25 minutes. First 10 minutes at gas 8/230°C/450°F, remainder at gas 6/200°C/400°F. (Hens are slightly smaller and usually give better results than cocks. Count 5 minutes more for a cock.)

**Woodcock:** 15 to 18 minutes at gas 8/230°C/450°F.

**Snipe:** 8 to 10 minutes at gas 9/260°C/500°F.


GARNISHES FOR ROASTS

With few exceptions, a single garnish will throw a roast most successfully into relief; a desultory collection of vegetables can only destroy the harmony. Tradition sanctions certain alliances: haricot (or flageolet) beans, parboiled little green beans – or a mixture of the two tossed with butter and chopped parsley at the last minute – with roast lamb; sliced apples sautéed in butter with pork; *gratin dauphinois* or Yorkshire pudding with beef; sorrel purée or buttered egg noodles with veal; lentil or chestnut purée with venison; potato crisps in some form with game birds; cabbage braised with an old partridge or pheasant to accompany young, roast partridge or pheasant.

Amongst potato *gratins*, the *gratin dauphinois* (a large, shallow *gratin* dish generously rubbed with garlic and left to dry, buttered, layered with thinly sliced, unrinsed potatoes, salt but no pepper, boiled milk poured in until barely visible, double cream spread over the surface, baked at gas 5/190°C/375°F for at least an hour or until the liquid is absorbed and the cream transformed into an undulating, golden-brown veil) may be the most versatile, but others are wonderfully adapted to particular roasts.

With lamb, pork, veal, chicken or hutch rabbit, serve thinly sliced, unrinsed potatoes and thinly sliced onions, salted, brought to the boil while stirring in an absolute minimum of water, spread into a *gratin* dish with their liquid and covered with shredded, butter-stewed sorrel that has been heavily creamed, baked like the *dauphinois*.

The following dish is astonishing with pheasant, partridge or guinea fowl, and indeed good with all roasts. Cut potatoes to spaghetti-like shreds in a mouli-julienne, rinse and dry in a towel, toss for a few seconds with plenty of butter over heat just to coat them, salt and press in two layers into a *gratin* dish with a layer of sliced truffles and 3 or 4 unpeeled garlic cloves scattered between. Bake for 40–45 minutes until the surface is delicately crisp and golden.

With venison, hare, lamb, veal or pork, try thinly sliced potatoes, rinsed and dried, and thinly sliced celeriac, both tossed in butter for a few seconds, layered, salted, with a layer of potatoes on the surface and baked for about 50 minutes.

Purées are good with meat roasts in particular. A purée of peeled broad beans, mature but still bright green beneath the skins, parboiled with a branch of winter savory for a few minutes until easily crushable, sieved, seasoned and rapidly reheated by beating with a wooden spoon over high heat, enough butter beaten in off the heat to loosen it to a creamy, nearly pourable consistency, goes particularly well with lamb, venison or hare. (Peeling the broad beans is tedious but the purée may be stretched by using it as a garnish for parboiled and butter-stewed artichoke bottoms.) Another good accompaniment for these roasts is a mixed purée of potatoes, garlic, onions, celeriac and either turnips or swedes, generously buttered at the last minute.

Little onions, unpeeled garlic cloves, artichoke hearts and a bouquet garni, a handful of shredded lettuce or sorrel scattered over, stewed, covered, in butter over very low heat forms a good basic stew to which other vegetables may be added at different times, depending on their cooking needs, or with which a pre-prepared vegetable (such as thinly sliced, rapidly sautéed courgettes; rapidly parboiled little *mange-tout* peas, green peas or broad beans; grilled, peeled, seeded and sliced sweet red peppers) may be tossed a couple of minutes before removing the stew from the heat and binding it with more butter. Serve this with veal, pork, lamb, duck or goose.

## WINES WITH ROASTS

Choose your wine carefully. Not that roasts are difficult, on the contrary; because they have in common direct, uncomplicated tastes, any roast may take its wine from a large spectrum, but this quality of loyal simplicity makes it the ideal companion to a complex wine whose finesse is too often destroyed in more exotic company.

Certain solidly constructed white wines can be very good with roast white meats and, perhaps, better than most reds when a fruit is present as with some pork roasts but, unless a menu is dedicated solely to white wines, the position of a roast on a menu usually imposes a red wine and there are many light-bodied, relatively non-tannic red wines which, served young and quite cool, will admirably play the same role.

Red wines and red meats or game provide the richest territory for specific alliances. Roast beef may be the most versatile of meats in the sense that any decent red wine is happy in its presence. For this reason, it may also be the only safe choice for a particularly difficult wine, a fragile old claret, for instance, lace-like in structure, whose bouquet has evolved into an intricate web of memories and associations that, without an alert and untroubled palate, will be dulled or may never be experienced. This, like preventative medicine, is a protective rather than a creative marriage.

In red wines that take age well, the fruity and herbal odours of youth are characteristically joined by autumnal fragrances and by animal essences, usually fresh meats at an intermediate stage, often evolving into distinct associations with game and sometimes, as with Burgundies, particularly the growths from around Gevrey-Chambertin and Morey-Saint-Denis, developing a delicately scatological nuance. It is with wines of this sort that still retain the structural force of youth while the bouquet has evolved to mature complexity that the most exciting associations are possible, associations in which the wine's bouquet recalls the character of the roast or in which the meat's flavour is complemented by the more elusive autumnal suggestions of decaying leaves, truffle or wild mushrooms which are usually present at the same time. These are the magical marriages by which the roast and the wine are each endowed with an extra dimension unsuspected in less inspired company. Châteauneuf-du-Pape acquires, with age, a gamey nose ideally suited to roast hare; roast lamb or fresh, unmarinated venison seem often to be a perfect choice for a 15- to 20-year-old Médoc from a good year, whereas I have known Saint Juliens, much older, in whose bouquets the *fumet* of freshly plucked partridge was so precise that it would be difficult to imagine anything but roast partridge as a partner; Hermitage, Côte Rôtie or the red wines from the Côte Chalonnaise or the Côte de Beaune are all, when a few years old, impeccable with lamb or beef roasts and, later, with grouse, pheasant or partridge and the association of a Chambertin or a Clos de la Roche with a roast woodcock is sublime.

# The Family of Stews

*(Stewing, poaching, braising, fricasseeing and boiling)*

## ELISABETH LAMBERT ORTIZ

### STEWING

No cooking method is as versatile or rewarding as that of stewing, a term that comes to us, about 1576, via Middle English from the Old French *étuve* and means a preparation of meat or poultry cooked slowly in a saucepan, usually with vegetables. It is an ancient technique and one of the forerunners of cooking as we know it today. In Neolithic times when women were creating the art of cooking, the meat brought in by the hunters was extremely tough and badly butchered. The meat or poultry, perhaps with pot herbs, was put into a couldron, covered with water, and suspended over a fire whose heat the cook could not control to any extent. Our stews still consist essentially of meat or poultry, covered with water or stock, accompanied by vegetables and seasonings and simmered over low heat until the meat or poultry is tender. It is the simplest method of all in this cooking family, and though it has become more sophisticated over the intervening centuries, it still reflects its original aim: long, slow cooking to tenderise tougher cuts of meat, or the more mature bird.

For successful stewing, heat must be even and gentle and the stewpot, casserole or saucepan must be a heavy one. Enamelled cast-iron saucepans or casseroles are admirable, though other heavy cookware, including special glass, is also good. The meat or poultry used should be of good quality and cut into even-sized pieces. Fowl or heavier birds, not young chickens, are the most suitable poultry. The best cuts of beef are chuck, blade, silverside, topside, rump, brisket or shin. Shoulder, neck and breast of veal, or lamb, may be used and almost any cut of pork can be stewed.

There are two kinds of stew, the white and the brown. In white stews the meat is put directly into the cooking liquid; in brown stews it is first sautéed in fat or oil, until lightly browned. Perhaps the best known of all white stews in the English-speaking world is Irish stew which consists of mutton, more usually lamb nowadays, potatoes and onions, simmered together. It can be an exquisite, or a very ordinary dish, according to the quality of the ingredients used, and the exactness of the technique employed. This is true of all stews which can be dull dishes or superb ones according to the cook. In Irish stew, where the pure flavours of lamb, onions and potatoes blend gently together, skimming to remove the fat, which is disagreeable, is important. I sometimes parcook the lamb with extra onions and water to cover for about 45 minutes, cool and refrigerate, then remove the hardened fat. I finish the cooking with more onions, potatoes and seasonings, skimming if necessary. Some cooks use whole as well as sliced potatoes, putting the sliced potatoes on the bottom of the pot so that they disintegrate, thickening the cooking liquid, while the small, whole potatoes covering the meat remain intact.

## Irish stew

| 1½ kg | 3 lb | potatoes, peeled and thickly sliced |
|---|---|---|
| 1½ kg | 3 lb | boned shoulder of lamb, cut into 5 cm/2 inch pieces, or best end of neck chops, trimmed and boned |
| 1 tbs chopped thyme and parsley, mixed | | |
| 1 kg | 2 lb | onions, thinly sliced |
| salt, freshly ground pepper | | |
| 450 ml | ¾ pint | water |
| Serves 6 to 8 | | |

In a heavy flameproof casserole make a layer of a third of the potatoes, then half the meat, half the herbs, and half the onions. Repeat with the rest of the meat, herbs, onions and potatoes, seasoning each layer with salt and pepper and ending with a layer of potatoes. Pour in the water, bring to a simmer on top of the stove, cover with aluminium foil and the lid and bake in a pre-heated slow oven (gas 2/150° C/300° F) for 2 hours, or simmer gently on top of the stove. Skim off any fat. Serve with small whole carrots, or red cabbage, or any green vegetable.

If preferred, make only one layer of meat starting with half the potatoes, half the onions, the meat and herbs, the rest of the onions and the potatoes.

## Navarin d'agneau
(Lamb stew with spring vegetables)

This is an excellent example of a brown stew.

| | | |
|---|---|---|
| 1½ kg | 3 lb | boneless shoulder of lamb cut into 5 cm/ 2 inch cubes |
| salt, freshly ground pepper | | |
| 4 tbs vegetable oil, or melted pork fat | | |
| 30 ml | 1 oz | butter |
| 1tbs finely chopped shallot or onion | | |
| 15 g | ½ oz | flour |
| 450 ml | ¾ pint | beef stock |
| ½ kg | 1 lb | tomatoes, peeled, seeded and chopped |
| 1 clove garlic, crushed | | |
| 1 bay leaf, sprig thyme, 2 sprigs parsley, tied with a piece of cotton | | |
| 6 medium potatoes, peeled | | |
| 6 medium carrots, scraped and quartered, or cut into olive shapes | | |
| 6 small turnips, peeled, quartered, or cut into olive shapes | | |
| 12 small white onions, peeled | | |
| 120 g | ¼ lb | shelled green peas |
| 120 g | ¼ lb | green beans, cut into 1½ cm/½ inch pieces |
| 1 tbs chives, finely chopped | | |
| 1 tbs parsley, finely chopped | | |
| Serves 6 | | |

Season the lamb with salt and pepper. In a large, heavy frying pan heat the oil and brown the lamb pieces lightly all over. Do this in batches, transferring the browned lamb to a heavy, flameproof casserole. Discard the fat in the frying pan and wipe it out with paper towels. Heat the butter and sauté the onion with the flour over low heat, stirring constantly with a wooden spoon until the mixture is golden brown. Stir in the beef stock, tomatoes and garlic, bring to a simmer, stirring, then pour into the casserole. Add the bay leaf, thyme and parsley. Cover the casserole with aluminium foil, then the lid and transfer to a pre-heated moderate oven (gas 4/180° C/350° F). At the end of 1 hour remove the casserole from the oven. Add the potatoes, carrots, turnips and onions and bring the liquid back to a simmer on top of the stove. Cover and return to the oven. Cook for 1 hour longer, or until both meat and vegetables are tender. Drop the peas and beans into briskly boiling salted water and simmer for 5 minutes. Drain. When ready to serve, lift the casserole out of the oven, add the peas and beans. Spoon some of the sauce over them, cover and cook on top of the stove over low heat for 5 minutes longer. Sprinkle with chives and parsley. Serve with crusty bread.

## POACHING

Stewing as a culinary discipline has well defined rules exemplified in the two stews given above, but the term to stew has a wider meaning and in a general sense includes poaching, boiling, braising and fricasseeing, all ways of creating, in a liquid medium, appetising dishes in almost infinite variety. An early refinement of stewing is poaching, where the temperature of the cooking liquid is accurately controlled and kept at what Escoffier called 'a boiling that does not boil', meaning a liquid whose temperature is just under the boiling point, where the cooking liquid does not move or bubble, but trembles gently. No form of cooking is as subtle as poaching, which can be used for meat, poultry, fish and shellfish, and for fruit. For this method use a pan into which the food fits comfortably and which is just deep enough for liquid to barely cover it; food is not fully immersed in liquid for poaching. The liquid should be well seasoned as it is important in flavouring the food. Vegetables and herbs appropriate to the food being poached are added – onions, garlic, carrots, leeks, celery, parsley, chervil, bay leaves and so on. Stock may be used instead of water and wine may be added. The following are two excellent examples of poaching.

## Poached chicken

| | | |
|---|---|---|
| 2 *medium carrots, scraped* | | |
| 2 *medium onions, peeled* | | |
| 3 *leeks, trimmed, washed and tied in a bundle* | | |
| 2 *stalks celery, trimmed* | | |
| *bouquet garni: 1 small bay leaf, 1 sprig thyme, 2 sprigs parsley, 2 cloves garlic, tied in a square of cheesecloth* | | |
| 2 *tsp salt* | | |
| 2 *litres* | 3½ *pints* | *water* |
| 1–1½ *kg* | 2–3 *lb* | *chicken* |
| *optional stuffing* | | |
| *Serves 4 to 6* | | |

In a saucepan, combine the carrots, onions, leeks, celery, bouquet garni, salt and water. Bring to a boil, lower the heat and simmer, covered, for 1 hour. Skim if necessary. Cool.

If the bird is to be stuffed, use any stuffing for roast chicken and truss the bird as usual. Truss the unstuffed bird. Place the bird, breast side up, in a closely fitting oval saucepan or flameproof casserole. Arrange the vegetables and bouquet garni around it. Pour the stock over, enough barely to cover. Bring the liquid to a simmer, skim, then reduce the heat so that the surface of the liquid merely trembles. Use asbestos mats if necessary to lower the heat. Poach for about 1 hour, or until the chicken is tender. Keep the bird warm while making the sauce, which may be a simple *velouté*, or *velouté* enriched into a *sauce suprême*, or a sauce *allemande* (also called *parisienne*). Lift the bird onto a warmed serving dish, remove the trussing strings and pour a little of the sauce over it. Serve the rest of the sauce in a sauce-boat. Accompany with rice. For a richer flavour, use chicken or a light veal stock instead of water as the poaching liquid.

## Poached sole

| butter | | |
|---|---|---|
| 1 tbs chopped shallots, spring onions, or onion | | |
| 6 fillets of sole weighing about 1 kg/2 lb | | |
| 300 ml | ½ pint | fish stock made from the bones of the fish and dry white wine |
| Serves 6 | | |

Butter a heavy frying pan or a fireproof baking dish large enough to hold the fish in one slightly overlapping layer. Sprinkle it with the shallots or onion. Arrange the fish on top. Cover with a piece of buttered parchment or cooking paper. Aluminium foil is not suitable as it discolours wine. Add the stock and bring to a simmer, cover with the lid and reduce the heat so that the liquid is just under a boil. Simmer for 10–12 minutes. The fish is done when it has lost its translucent look. The fish may be cooked in a pre-heated moderate oven (gas 4/180°C/350°F) after the liquid is brought to a simmer on top of the stove.

When the fish is cooked, lift it out onto a warmed serving dish, cover and keep warm while making a sauce.

This method is suitable for any firm-fleshed, fine-grained, non-oily fish. Coarse-grained fish tend to break up when poached.

### BOILING

The term boiling is a misnomer, though it was probably used in its exact sense in primitive times when cooking temperatures could not be accurately controlled. Boiled dishes are not boiled, they are simmered. Water boils on reaching 100° C/212° F at sea level. It simmers at 82°C/180° F. Food is immersed in a generous quantity of seasoned liquid and cooked until tender at a gentle simmer with an occasional bubble reaching the surface. Tougher cuts of meat and older birds respond to this cooking

method. The most famous of all the 'boiled' dishes are the
*pot-au-feu* and the *poule-au-pot* which result in boiled beef
and boiled chicken as well as soup, which is served separately with the vegetables that accompany the meat and
poultry in the pot. The soup may be used as the basis of
other soups, and the meat or poultry may be served with
various sauces such as horseradish or mustard, or used as
the basis of other dishes – for example lamb or chicken may
be used for curry.

Most countries have favourite boiled dishes – the *san-
cochos* of South America and the Spanish-speaking islands
of the Caribbean where meat and/or poultry are cooked
with a large number of root vegetables; Irish corned beef
and cabbage; the New England boiled dinner, also made
with corned (salted) beef, and Jewish boiled beef.

## Boiled beef

This is a very simple boiled beef recipe for which a number
of cuts of lean, boneless beef can be used. Boned ribs,
chuck, rolled silverside, topside or top rump are all suitable.

| 1½ kg | 3 lb | *piece lean, boneless beef* |
|---|---|---|
| 1 medium carrot, scraped and diced | | |
| 2 stalks celery, diced | | |
| 1 large onion, quartered | | |
| 1 parsnip, peeled and diced | | |
| 1 white turnip, peeled and diced | | |
| 1 bay leaf | | |
| 1 tsp salt | | |
| 6 peppercorns | | |
| 250 g | 8 oz | *tomatoes, peeled, seeded and chopped or use tinned* |
| 2 litres | 3½ pints | *water or beef stock* |
| Serves 6 | | |

Combine all the ingredients in a large heavy saucepan, bring to a simmer over low heat and skim until the liquid is clear. Cover and cook at a gentle simmer for about 2 hours or until the beef is tender. Lift out the beef on to a warmed serving platter. Remove the trussing strings if the beef has been tied, and carve into thick slices. Serve with horseradish, or mustard, and, if liked, dill pickles. Accompany the beef with boiled potatoes, tossed in butter and chopped parsley. Strain the cooking liquid and use as stock, or use it with the vegetables as a foundation for a soup.

## BRAISING

Braising is a far more sophisticated departure from the original simple boiling and stewing of meat. Tender cuts of meat and young birds are as well suited to braising as tougher cuts or more mature birds. Meat, poultry or fish for braising are usually not cut up and may be larded or marinated. The food to be cooked is first browned in fat, then placed in a buttered casserole on a bed of aromatic vegetables (onions, carrots, celery) as well as herbs and other flavourings, and moistened with enough liquid (wine, stock or tinned tomatoes) to half-cover the meat or poultry. Frequent basting keeps the food moist. During cooking the liquid reduces and its flavours intensify, giving a rich sauce to accompany moist and succulent meat or poultry. A braise may be cooked in the oven or on top of the stove and some braised meats may be served cold as well as hot, *bœuf à la mode*, for instance where the clarified sauce makes a coating of jelly for the beef.

## Braised beef

| 2 kg | 4 lb | piece boneless rump, silverside or topside of beef |
|------|------|---------------------------------------------------|
| 10 strips larding pork | | |
| salt, freshly ground pepper | | |
| 1 medium onion, coursely chopped | | |
| 1 medium carrot, scraped and sliced | | |
| 2 cloves garlic, chopped | | |
| 2 small stalks celery, coursely chopped | | |
| 2 sprigs parsley | | |
| sprig thyme | | |
| 1 bay leaf | | |
| 450 ml | ¾ pint | dry red wine |
| 50 ml | 2 fl oz | cognac or other brandy |
| 3 tbs melted pork fat or vegetable oil | | |
| 30 g | 1 oz | butter |
| 1 pig's foot, split | | |
| 800 ml | 1½ pints | beef stock |
| Serves 8 to 10 | | |

Lard the beef through the centre with the strips of larding pork and tie it with string about every 5 cm/2 inches, or have the butcher do it. Season the meat with salt and pepper and place it in a large bowl with the onion, carrot, garlic, celery, parsley, thyme and bay leaf. Pour in the wine and cognac, cover and marinate in the refrigerator over-night, turning the meat once or twice. When ready to cook, remove the meat from the marinade and pat it dry with paper towels.

In a heavy flameproof casserole heat the pork fat or vegetable oil and brown the beef all over. Lift out the beef and set it aside. Pour out the browning fat. Add the butter. Strain the marinade and add the vegetables from the marinade. Cook, stirring, over moderate heat for a few minutes. Add the beef, the pig's foot, the marinade and enough stock to come about two thirds of the way up the meat. Bring to a simmer on top of the stove, cover with foil, then the lid and put into a pre-heated moderate oven (gas 4/180° C/350° F) and simmer for about 4 hours, turning two or three times during cooking. While the meat is braising, prepare the garnish.

| | | |
|---|---|---|
| 75 g | 2½ oz | *butter* |
| 24 *small white onions* | | |
| 1 *tbs sugar* | | |
| 1 kg | 2 lb | *carrots, scraped and quartered* |
| *salt, pepper* | | |
| *water* | | |

In a saucepan heat 45 g/1½ oz butter and add the onions. Sauté over moderate heat until they are lightly browned, rolling them in the pan to brown evenly. Pour in enough of the brown stock used for the beef (about 125 ml/¼ pint) to cover and simmer slowly, covered, until they are tender – about 30 minutes. Set aside until ready to add to the beef.

In another saucepan combine 30 g/1 oz butter, the sugar, carrots, salt, pepper and enough water to cover (about 300 ml/½ pint). Bring to a simmer and cook, covered, over moderate heat until the carrots are tender and the liquid has evaporated – about 30 minutes. Set aside until ready to add to the beef.

When the beef is tender, remove it to a warmed platter and keep it warm in the turned-off oven. Remove the strings.

Skim off the fat from the braising liquid. Strain the liquid, pressing down to remove all the juices from the vegetables. Discard the vegetables. Return the liquid to the casserole and reduce it over high heat to about 600 ml/1 pint. Taste for seasoning and add salt and pepper if necessary. If the sauce seems thin, stir in 1 tbs cornflour mixed with 2 tbs water and simmer until the sauce is thickened – about 2 minutes. Add the onions and carrots and simmer just long enough to heat them through. Arrange the onions and carrots round the beef. Spoon a little of the sauce over the beef and serve the rest in a sauce-boat.

## FRICASSEES

For all practical purposes the blanquettes and the fricassees belong with the braises, and are dishes in which the sauce is thickened with egg yolks and cream. Veal and chicken are the principal meats used in these 'white' dishes. In a blanquette the food is put directly into the cooking liquid, in a fricassee it is first sautéed, without colouring, in butter. The sauce that turns a braise into a fricassee is made by lightly beating together egg yolks and cream, which are then combined with the strained braising liquid, poured over the meat and cooked, over very low heat, just until the sauce has thickened lightly and the flavours are blended. It must not even come to a simmer, but remain as a poaching liquid does, just under a boil. It will then be smooth and creamy. If it boils, the sauce curdles. It is very rich and unctuous. The following recipe explains the technique.

## *Veal fricassee*

| $1\frac{1}{2}$ kg | 3 lb | boneless veal, cut into 3 cm/1½inch cubes |
|---|---|---|
| salt, freshly ground pepper | | |
| a pinch of grated nutmeg | | |
| 90 g | 3 oz | butter |
| 1 tbs flour | | |
| 1 litre | 1½ pints | white veal stock, chicken stock or water |
| bouquet garni: 2 sprigs parsley, 1 sprig thyme, bay leaf, tied with a piece of cotton | | |
| 2 medium carrots, scraped and cut into 2½ cm/1 inch pieces | | |
| 1 medium onion, stuck with a clove | | |
| 250 g | 8 oz | button mushrooms, wiped and trimmed |
| 2 tbs lemon juice | | |

| 125 ml | $\frac{1}{4}$ pint | water |
| --- | --- | --- |
| 16 small onions | | |
| 3 egg yolks | | |
| 250 ml | 8 fl oz | double cream |
| Serves 6 | | |

Season the veal pieces with salt, pepper and nutmeg. Heat 45 ml/1½ oz of the butter in a heavy frying pan and sauté the veal over moderate heat until barely golden on all sides. Do not let it colour. Sprinkle with the flour, stirring with a wooden spoon to mix. Pour in the veal stock and simmer, stirring, until the liquid has thickened lightly. Transfer the contents of the frying pan to a flameproof casserole. Add the bouquet garni, the carrot and onion, cover and simmer over very low heat for 1½ hours or until the veal is tender.

While the veal is cooking put the mushrooms into a saucepan with the lemon juice and water. Season with salt and pepper, add 15 g/½ oz butter and simmer, uncovered, for 2 minutes. Set aside.

Put the onions with the remaining 30 g/1 oz of butter into a pan large enough to hold them in a single layer, season with salt and pepper, cover and cook over low heat, shaking the pan from time to time to stop the onions from sticking, for about 15 minutes, or until they are tender but not browned. Set aside.

When the veal is cooked, lift it out of the casserole into a bowl, add the mushrooms and onions, cover and keep warm. Strain the liquid in the casserole. Pick out the carrot slices and add to the veal. Discard the onion and bouquet garni. Return the liquid to the casserole. There should be 500 ml/¾ pint. If there is more liquid than this, reduce it over high heat. Beat the egg yolks with the cream in a bowl and whisk in a cup of the hot liquid from the casserole. Pour the mixture into the casserole and cook, stirring, over very low heat for 1 minute. Add the veal, onions, mushrooms and carrot and cook over very low heat, stirring gently with a wooden spoon until the sauce is blended – 1 or 2 minutes. Do not let the sauce boil. Serve with rice.

None of the cooking techniques in what I have called the family of stews is hard to master. The differences between a stew and a braise, a poaching and a fricassee, are not great. For the most part it is a question of the amount and type of liquid used, the vegetables and seasonings added, and the temperature at which the dish is cooked. Attention to detail is what matters. A poaching, for example, must never reach a simmer, and a dish to be simmered must be maintained at the correct temperature. This is very easy to do, but the rules must be observed. Then a whole world of delectable dishes is available to the cook. Since the finer cuts of meat are not necessary, the dishes are as modestly priced as they are delicious, a considerable advantage.

# Fats: Which to Use When

## MARGARET PATERSON

Looking round the range of fats in any good grocer's or supermarket can be confusing unless one knows what one wants. Many shoppers are probably so influenced by price, flavour, convenience and/or health and diet that through sheer habit they buy the same kinds week after week without always being aware of how other fats might improve their cooking – and eating – if only they knew more about them.

Not everyone, for instance, knows the advantages of a soft lard over traditional lards; why for certain purposes one type of oil may be preferable to another, why dripping can be such a pitfall, why some recipes cal for unsalted rather than salted butter, when and why margarine can or cannot be substituted for butter.

In writing about each type of fat, I have three main aims: first, to explain how and why for certain purposes that fat may be superior to another. Secondly, because not everyone can afford the most suitable fat or perhaps because this is not in the larder when wanted, to list the possible uses of each, even if that fat would not be the ideal choice. Thirdly, to try to create variety, by drawing attention to fats of recent as well as of ancient origin. Information of this nature is not normally to be found in a recipe book. This chapter is intended to fill the gap. At the end of the chapter I have included notes on saturated and unsaturated fats for those who are concerned about coronary disease.

BUTTER

A basic ingredient of the best chefs and cooks. Should the purse allow, I would use butter, when appropriate, in preference to any other fat. Where flavour and textures are concerned, there is not another to match its combined qualities: not only has it a natural and delicate flavour of its own but, as a cooking medium, it often gives a memorable nutty flavour as well as an unrivalled golden colour to foods cooked in it. Butter is irreplaceable in certain classic dishes. Its major limitation is that it burns at a lower temperature than many other fats. (But see Elizabeth David's chapter on clarified butter.)

Other good, but less obvious, qualities of butter are:
– that it is more easily digested than various other fats and is a good source of vitamins A and D.
– the way it melts at mouth temperature, the flavour and feeling of it on the tongue being quite different from those of margarine. This explains, for instance, why thinly cut brown bread spread generously with butter makes such a perfect accompaniment to something like smoked fish.
– the way it absorbs flavours and colours. It has no equal for savoury butters, hard sauces and butter-based cake icings. Made with butter, these icings spread easily and smoothly, or can be piped in clearly defined shapes.

## A few general tips

1. Salted butter goes brown and burns at a lower temperature than saltless, thus discolouring anything cooked in it. This is one reason why some recipes call for unsalted or clarified butter – that which you have de-salted – because a good colour and flavour are basic to success. It is also why you shouldn't sprinkle salt over foods you are frying in butter, because salt makes them stick to the pan as well as burn more readily. It is much easier, and because of wastage less costly, to buy unsalted butter than to clarify salted.

2. Butter tastes best when chilled, so for the table have it slightly chilled if you can: put your pats etc. straight into iced water, then cover and refrigerate until needed.

3. When a recipe tells you to melt butter, it *means* melt, not heat it. It is usually best melted over minimum heat because if overheated it separates and goes oily, and then will not amalgamate properly with other ingredients.

4. To sauté foods, you should ideally us unsalted butter, or this with a small proportion of olive oil: the oil allows the butter to reach a higher temperature without burning. The butter must be *hot* – the appearance of foam indicates the right moment to start cooking. As the butter melts, there is no foam and nothing would cook in it but, as it heats, the liquids in the butter begin to evaporate, making it foam. It is as the foam subsides, when the liquids have just evaporated, that you should add the food. Should you miss this stage, the butter starts to change colour and the hotter it becomes, the darker brown it turns, until at 137° C/278° F it burns.

5. The cheapest butter is almost always better for cooking than the most expensive margarine.

## When butter is best, and why

**Sauces.** Sauces made with butter, when appropriate, are usually better than those same sauces made with margarine, or any other fat. Butter's special properties, however it is incorporated, are basic to many of the most delicate sauces served with vegetables, fish, meat and poultry. Together with flour, for instance, butter may form the roux which, when cooked, acquires a rather nutty flavour as well as controlling a sauce's essential colour. Alternatively, butter may be added to the sauce at the last, to give a smoothness, gloss and taste unobtainable with other fats. For some dishes, such as asparagus, butter is the sauce; for a fine plain dish such as grilled rump steak or Dover sole, savoury butters (e.g. *maître d'hôtel*, mustard butter) are a form of instant sauce, butter always being the perfect fat both because of its own flavour and for the way in which it absorbs other flavours.

In tepid sauces, such as *hollandaise* or *béarnaise*, butter is the only fat which will emulsify with the coagulated egg yolks to make the smooth, shiny and rich accompaniment for which qualities these sauces are so famous.

Besides the avoury sauces, there are, of course, the sweet: made with margarine, a butterscotch sauce for instance, tends to separate, while for hard sauces such as brandy or rum butter, margarine does not absorb a flavour in the same way as does butter – and nor is the taste as delicate.

**Soups.** Many of the finest soups depend on butter for their delicate and often subtle flavour, teir colour and their texture. Even the simplest vegetable purée soup made with butter is in a different category from the same kind made with most oils or with margarine. If butter seems an extravagance, remember that you will only need about 25 g/1 oz for six to eight servings so, per person, the saving is trivial.

**Omelettes and scrambled eggs.** For traditional flavour and creamy texture butter is a must, margarine a bad substitute.

**Vegetables.** With vegetables, butter is used largely for flavour, including that which it imparts to a food itself, so you can quite often use margarine or oil – olive oil is excellent for certain dishes – or perhaps some other fat as long as you don't expect the end product to taste the same. Alternatively, if you can afford to be extravagant, fresh or soured cream can, on occasion, even be superior to butter.

**Fish, meat and poultry.** To sauté or shallow fry small pieces of fish or the most choice and tender cuts of meat like fillet steaks or chicken breasts, butter gives a sweetness unmatched by other fats. If you grill or roast certain foods in butter they acquire gloss as well as taste. (Oil, lard or a white cooking fat can often be substituted, but the result is not the same.) Here for example is a delicious way to roast a turkey in butter. The butter muslin absorbs the fat, only gradually letting it drip down into the tin – so, amongst other benefits, there's no oven cleaning afterwards.

## *To roast a turkey in butter*

1. Put a good tablespoon of oil into a large roasting tin and grease all surfaces well.

2. Rub the prepared (stuffed, trussed) turkey all over (except underneath) with salt, to make the skin crisp, and put the bird in the roasting tin. Spread liberally with about 80 g/3 oz well softened butter, then cover with a doubled piece of butter muslin, cut to the right size to protect bird completely (about 45 cm/$\frac{1}{2}$ yard).

3. Roast at the bottom of a pre-heated slowish oven (gas 3/160° C/325° F) and baste hourly over the muslin, which stays on throughout cooking time. Allow 45 minutes per kg/20 minutes per lb *stuffed weight* for a bird over 5$\frac{1}{2}$ kg/12 lb, a good 5 minutes more per kg/2 or 3 minutes more per lb for a smaller bird. Test for tenderness half to three quarters of an hour before cooking time is up.

**Pastry.** Flavour is an important function of butter in pastry-making, while its plasticity and waxiness ensure its even distribution in a dough. The method by which you make the various types of pastry is designed to give the required shortness, flakiness and/or leaf-like layers.

In certain kinds of pastry, butter plays a particular role, in others margarine is often used. Those always made with butter are:

*choux* – to give a golden, crisp, yet tender shell, and a delicate flavour not acquired with margarine, but always associated with this pastry.

*genoese* – to give flavour, richness of colour and, particularly, to keep the crumb moist and fresh.

*French flan (pâte sucrée)* – for a short texture and a rich flavour.

*puff* – for even distribution of the fat, and vital to the flavour, leafy character and golden colour of this pastry. You cannot substitute margarine here, any more than you can substitute plain household flour for strong flour.

**Rich doughs.** In some, butter is irreplaceable: the flakiness of *croissants*, the smooth texture of Danish pastries, the lightness of a *savarin* or of *brioches* simply cannot be obtained with any other fat.

**Sandwiches.** Butter triumphs over margarine in every way: it is the perfect harmoniser between bread and any filling; it never has that gooey texture of margarine; it gives the best flavour. Liberally buttered sandwiches taste better, keep fresh longer, won't absorb moisture from a filling and will dry out less should freezing be necessary. For good measure, butter blends almost to a paste if mixed with a purée of fish, meat or poultry so, when time is at a premium, all spreading can be done in one operation.

**Cakes.** Butter is usually superior to margarine or oil because the flavour is better, the texture is generally better and, unless a cake is to be eaten up on the day of baking, it will keep fresh and moist longer. When making a Christmas or wedding cake, which must be kept if to mature properly, it is a complete waste of time and other expensive ingredients to economise by using margarine. (But see p. 182.)

**Biscuits.** Butter has special 'shortening' qualities so, for texture as well as flavour, margarine is usually a bad substitute. (Given a strong flavour like ginger or mixed spice, you can more easily get away with margarine.)

## MARGARINE

Besides having a multitude of uses in its own right, margarine can sometimes be used where butter has been called for. Some modern margarines which attempt to bridge the gap between butter and hard margarine may, in some circumstances, be hardly distinguishable from butter: I find it difficult, for instance, to spot the difference between one particular brand and butter in a jacket potato, but not difficult in something delicately flavoured like shortbread.

Margarines vary so much in flavour, quality, texture, cholesterol content and cost that it can be puzzling to know which brands are best to meet particular needs. The top-quality brands are a very superior fat, and their cost is usually determined by the oils and fats used. All the oils are fully refined, but some sources that can be used are cheaper than others, and a greater proportion of these cheaper oils are present in the cheaper brands. Edible vegetable oils are the more expensive variety. They are more costly than marine oils and animal fats, so products made only with vegetable oils – such as sunflower margarines – are usually among the more expensive. Legally, all table margarines must conform to certain nutritional standards, which accounts for a weight-watcher's fat, which does not conform precisely to the regulations, being called a 'low fat spread', not a margarine.

The difference between a soft and a hard margarine is that soft products contain a higher proportion of oils which are liquid at room temperature than the harder products. Although their uses often overlap, one type is sometimes unquestionably better than the other: in pastry, for instance, or when the fat has to be rubbed or rolled in, soft margarines are *too* soft. Unlike a soft lard which is primarily intended for pastry-making, a soft margarine makes a dough difficult to manipulate and won't trap as much air, so the pastry isn't as light. (Their extreme softness is obvious in the way they are packed: soft margarines come in tubs, so they can't run away, but soft lards are simply parchment-wrapped.) On the other hand, soft margarine is marvellous for making an all-in-one mixture, the modern version of a creamed mixture: in less time than it takes to gather together the ingredients, you can mix and have a cake ready for the oven or a pudding for the steamer. I like to use all the ingredients at room temperature because I get the best results this way, but if you use an exceptionally soft margarine (like a sunflower margarine) it is better used refrigerated. This is because if it is used at room temperature and you beat it too long with an electric mixer, it may 'oil', spoiling the end result.

## An all-in-one mixture

| 100 g | 4 oz | self-raising flour |
|---|---|---|
| 1 level tsp baking powder | | |
| ½ level tsp salt | | |
| 100 g | 4 oz | soft margarine |
| 100 g | 4 oz | sugar, preferably caster |
| 2 eggs | | |
| flavouring, e.g. about 1 tbs coffee essence, or the finely grated rind of ½–1 lemon or orange | | |

Sift together the flour, baking powder and salt. (You need baking powder as well as self-raising flour in order to get a good rise.) Beat all the ingredients together for a minute or two in a mixing bowl until light, fluffy and completely blended.

To bake a cake, use a slow/moderate oven (gas 3/160° C/325° F). To steam a pudding, allow 1¾–2 hours, or until firm; only 1–1¼ hours for half quantities.

I am less enthusiastic about all-in-one pastry and all-in-one white sauce made with soft margarine, so am omitting the details. The results seem to me inferior to pastry and sauce made in the conventional ways, and the time saved, if any, is minimal.

## OILS

Cooking oils are less versatile than those fats which can be used in both solid and liquid form, but are the only choice for dishes where other fats of similar temperature would congeal. We wouldn't, for example, contemplate making French dressing with butter, or a marinade with dripping. As most oils solidify at a considerably lower temperature than other fats, this is the fat to use when a mixture must remain completely liquid. This explains why it is better to fry or roast in oil dishes which are to be served cold: a roast chicken for example, or fried *canapés* for buffet snacks.

Oils naturally have a multitude of uses besides these: some kinds (see the list below) are excellent for deep as well as shallow frying and if for some reason or other you don't want to fry with butter when it is called for, oil is often the best substitute. Mixed with butter to fry or sauté foods – approximately 2–4 teaspoons of oil to 50 g/2 oz/4 tbs butter – it allows the butter to reach a higher temperature without burning. This is an advantage should the food you are cooking need more than just a few minutes in the frying pan.

Oils can also be used to sweat sliced onions or shallots, to make roux for soups and sauces, in certain batters and, if you like the results (which I do not) in cakes and scones.

A solid vegetable oil, grated rather than rubbed in (p. 189), brings variety to pastry.

Some kinds of oil are more suitable than others for particular dishes, their flavours, or lack of it, usually being the deciding factor. The flavour of an oil is to some extent dependent on the refining process: the more highly refined, the less flavour and odour it will have, which explains why for most purposes it pays to buy a good oil.

The level of refining is set by a manufacturer's specifications, so naturally even the same types of oil can and do vary. An unbranded supermarket corn oil, for instance, is not necessarily of the same high quality as a branded corn oil.

Amongst the many uses for oil, 1 or 2 teaspoons mixed with an egg yolk makes an excellent coating when 'egg and breadcrumbing' foods: not only is it economical because the yolk goes further, but the emulsion so formed gives a thin, even coating which is easily brushed on. Although I usually prefer melted lard, oil is also good for greasing bread or cake tins, pudding basins or baking sheets, since it is pure as well as easy to brush on. For any form of meringue, I prefer oiled greaseproof paper on oiled baking sheets to anything else, because it is better to use a vegetable rather than a meat fat. When greasing tins and lining for Christmas and wedding cakes, oil is as successful as melted lard.

Quite apart from its uses in cooking, oil is a tonic to all wooden kitchen equipment: treat your salad bowl, servers, cheeseboard or whatever to a shiny new face with a tissue dipped lightly in oil.

Oils should be kept in a coolish, dark place. So stored they should generally keep, unopened, for six months or more. If oils go cloudy when very cold, simply stand the bottle in a jug of hot water until clear again.

## Corn oil

Pure corn oil is bland in flavour, thus making it a very versatile product. You can use it in almost any recipe which calls for oil: salad dressings, marinades, shallow or deep-fat frying, roux-based soups and sauces, and in a wide variety of baking. Because they do not like the fruity flavour of olive oil (or perhaps because they haven't found an olive oil they like), some people prefer corn to olive oil even in mayonnaise, completely tasteless though the mayonnaise is.

The recommended temperature for deep-fat frying with pure corn oil is 190° C/375° F. The smoke point is 227° C/440° F and the flash point 300° C/575° F.

Pure corn oil contains no cholesterol and is high in polyunsaturated fats.

## Groundnut (peanut) oil

Different grades of groundnut oil vary considerably, but at its best it is light and bland in flavour and thought by some people to be excellent for salad dressings. It is widely used by manufacturers, blended with other oils to make what we buy as 'vegetable oils', and also in prepared dressings etc.

## Olive oils

Olive oil is as essential to cooking as butter if you enjoy good food. 'Virgin' oils are the finest – delicate and aromatic, giving flavour to anything made with them. For mayonnaise and salad dressings, this oil has no equal, unless of course you dislike its fruity taste. Use it also for marinades, casseroles, shallow frying, sautéing, grilling and roasting, to pour over pasta or to toss with vegetables. Do *not* use it for deep-fat frying because of its low smoke point: if heated to the temperature necessary to fry foods in deep fat, it will break down and give off a blue vapour.

The best olive oils are always expensive because they are so costly to produce. Like wines, they vary with climate, country (and even area) of origin and from year to year. Many different varieties of olives are grown for oil, so the range of oils is wide. They vary in flavour, colour, aroma, consistency and character and come mainly from France and Italy (these two considered the best), Spain, Greece (whose oils tend to be thick and heavy), Turkey, Morocco and Tunisia. Spain is known for its oil 'lake', but Spanish oils are heavier and more fruity than the French and Italian, generally making food cooked in them less digestible. It may take time, therefore, to find your ideal oil, because even if you can afford the very finest you may prefer the flavour of another which comes from a different area or country.

Good wine merchants will e as selective in their choice of an olive oil as of wine and will sell an oil infinitely superior to anything obtainable at a chemist's – even though the latter is labelled 'pure olive oil': for medical use, flavour and aroma don't matter, whereas purity does. You may also find fine oils in health-food shops, delicatessens and any shops selling top-quality groceries. Supermarkets are more likely to sell a pure but blended oil (not a virgin oil), because it will be cheaper.

French and Italian labelling laws ensure that the customer may know exactly what he or she is getting because, even among virgin oils, there are several qualities, depending on their acidity. As few shop assistants will have the knowledge to advise you in detail, be your own expert and learn to interpret the label yourself:

**Virgin oil.** This is cold-pressed ('first pressing'), the first to be squeezed from the olives. It is natural and pure, without further treatment and without the admixture of any other oil, of whatever origin. Besides stating 'huile d'olive' and 'vierge' (virgin), the label must give further qualifications to indicate the quality. The grades are:

| French oils | Italian oils | Maximum allowance of oleic acid |
|---|---|---|
| 1. Vierge 'Extra' | Olio 'Extra' Vergine | 1% |
| 2. Vierge 'Fine' | Olio 'Soprafino' Vergine | 1.5% |
| 3. Vierge 'Semi-fine' or 'Courante' | Olio 'Fino' Vergine | 3% |
| 4. — | Olio Vergine | 4% |

In addition, a label may also give a grower's name, the site of pressing, the method of pressing and a descriptive adjective such as *'fruitée'* or *'douce'*.

If you buy one of these oils you can be sure of getting a genuine natural product. My own favourite is a 'Fine' virgin oil from Provence, 'Emile Martin'. To me a flavour I like is more important than a particular degree of acidity.

**Refined olive oils (Huiles d'olive raffinées).** These are obtained from the refining of oils which fail to qualify for the grades of virgin oil given above, either because of defective flavour or excessive acidity. The residual dryish pulp from the first pressing is pressed again ('second pressing'), this time using heat, to yield a fattier and more acid oil which is often blended with first-pressing oil to make commercial, branded, but still pure olive oils of a standard flavour (if any) and quality.

From the health angle, virgin (cold-pressed) olive oil, when eaten uncooked as in salad dressings, is one of the world's most nutritious foods. Of all fats it is the most easily digested, and the closest in chemical composition to the fat in mother's milk. It is also slightly laxative and full of valuable mineral salts and vitamins. It is only cooked for gourmet reasons and is not harmful to those with heart problems, because it is low in saturated fats and rich in unsaturated (see p. 198).

Although at their best in the first year, good olive oils will keep a long time if properly stored. Choose a coolish, dark or dimly lit place because they are sensitive to extremes of heat and cold, and also to light – one obvious advantage of a canned oil over a bottled. (Cold will make the oil congeal and too much heat or light can adversely affect flavour and colour.) Once opened, olive oil will still keep for months in such conditions, longer if there is not a large head-space in the can or bottle.

It is not necessarily an economy to buy a larger quantity

of olive oil than you are likely to want. Any surplus will in time go rancid, and don't forget that a large container is more difficult to pour from.

Table olives grow on different kinds of trees, specially developed to produce large, fleshy olives.

## Rapeseed oil

This has rather taken the place of soya oil in the manufacture of blended cooking oils because rape is now grown more widely in Europe.

## Safflower oil

This is little used in the UK, mainly because of its cost, but it has a bland flavour which makes it a versatile product. It is extremely rich in polyunsaturates, so is usually to be found in health-food shops.

## Sesame oil

Like safflower oil, sesame oil is not widely used in the UK, though it has been known for thousands of years in the Far East. It is used in oriental cooking, giving an attractive nutty flavour to food cooked in it. It is expensive compared with most other similar oils, but doesn't easily go rancid – a great asset in hot countries.

## Soya oil

The oil made from the soya bean is one of the cheapest there is. It has rather a marked 'backtaste', a flavour associated with soya which is difficult to diffuse, even in refining. Pure soya has its limitations, therefore, although it is used in many blended cooking oils.

## Sunflower oil

High in polyunsaturates, so for those with heart problems this is a safe choice in any recipe calling for oil – or for that matter, as a possible substitute for other fats. Sunflower oil lacks the flavour of a virgin olive oil, but is good for deep-fat as well as shallow frying and has a highish smoke point.

## Vegetable oils

Usually blends of various oils selected by a manufacturer. They may include sunflower, groundnut, soya and rapeseed, but not usually corn because of its cost. Blended oils aren't necessarily highly refined as this would add to their cost. Some vegetable oils may be restricted largely to frying or roasting as their backtaste would be unacceptable mixed or cooked in things.

## Walnut oil

Use for salad dressings, not for cooking. It has a distinctive nutty flavour as you would expect, but does not keep as long as most oils.

## Solid vegetable oil

This is, of course, quite unsuitable for traditional oil-based things like dressings and marinades because it solidifies when cold, but it has many other uses. For those unfamiliar with this fairly recent addition to the larder, a few tips may be helpful.

1. It will keep at least six months without going rancid if correctly stored, i.e. properly wrapped, in a refrigerator or cool, dry larder.

2. Used refrigerated, the oil is difficult to cut because excessively brittle but, if you need to grate it (in a mouli-grater for speed), it is much easier to handle.

3. It is excellent for deep-fat (and shallow) frying: you can use and re-use it for months because of its keeping qualities – as long as you strain it after use, preferably through butter muslin; it is almost odourless and flavourless; its smoke point is fairly high (approximately 220° C/425° F), as is its flash point (approximately 320° C/610° F); compared with most liquid oils, it leaves a much less rubbery (and difficult to clean off) deposit on the pan; it is less costly than many other fats you might use.

4. When melted, a 500 g/1.1 lb packet of oil equals approximately 550 ml/1 pint liquid oil.

5. It is safer and more convenient than a liquid oil for campers and caravanners.

6. Grated, this oil is a good substitute for suet, should you not have or never eat suet. Use the same quantity as you would of suet to make stuffings, shortcrust-type pastry (see below), mincemeat or a Christmas pudding (neither *quite* as good as with suet I find). Use only half the quantity to make suetcrust-type pastry (see below) for things like dumplings or a steak and kidney pudding.

7. If on the wrapper it is claimed that a pure vegetable oil is 100% pure without additives of any kind, this is a versatile and useful fat for vegetarians. The nature of the oil is not disclosed to anyone.

8. Because of its vegetable origin, it is low in cholesterol (0.003% compared with lard at 0.1% and butter at 0.18% but, being a *solid* oil, it is high in saturated fat (see p. 199).

## Shortcrust-type pastry

| | | |
|---|---|---|
| 250 g | 8 oz | *plain flour* |
| 1 *level tsp salt* | | |
| 125 g | 4 oz | *chilled solid oil, grated* |
| *water, to mix – more than for ordinary shortcrust* | | |

Sieve flour and salt together, then stir in the grated oil. Mix to a dry dough with water (its texture resembles suetcrust) and continue as for shortcrust, allowing rather longer to bake.

I find the result rather good: the top of a pie crust is golden and unusually crunchy, the underpart rather heavy but pleasantly so. For dishes like a plate pie or a quiche or flan, where there is an inner or lower layer of pastry, the ratio of the doughy part to the crunchy is unacceptably high unless the pastry is rolled very thin. If too thin, it may burn before a filling is cooked though, so beware.

## Suetcrust-type pastry

| 250 g | 8 oz | self-raising flour |
|---|---|---|
| 1 level tsp salt | | |
| 65 g | 2 oz | chilled solid oil, grated |
| water, to mix to a dry dough | | |

Make and cook exactly as ordinary suetcrust pastry.

I find the result both surprising and excellent. Even for a steak and kidney pudding, it could deceive anyone but the cook – and it's lighter and more digestible.

### LARD

Lard is the melted and purified fat of a pig. It is a fat I would never be without. Although top-quality compound white cooking fats undoubtedly have their merits and can be used in place of it, I like lard more because I think it gives better results, particularly in pastry and bread. It is also simple to use, whatever you are doing with it.

What kind of lard to buy though? Just as butter, olive oils and other fats may vary according to the country and area of origin, so, more surprisingly, do lards. The degree of hardness or softness also varies widely, depending not only on the climate in which pigs are reared, but also on their diet. While the best traditional lards are certainly pure and almost flavourless, the one real drawback of frying with this fat is its unpleasant smell when heated. There is now, however, a 100% pure and super-refined soft lard which has several advantages over hard lards. It is completely odourless in cooking, as well as having a bland taste. It is pre-creamed, so chilling has a minimal effect on its texture, and it is soft enough to roll out or rub in direct from the refrigerator, consequently making very light pastry. (It is primarily intended for pastry-making.) It has a higher smoke point and flash point than less pure lards, which makes it marginally safer for deep-fat frying. (Fats will burst into flame spontaneously above varyinggiven temperatures.)

## Some further hints about lard

1. Lard can be heated to a much higher temperature than butter without burning. It is hot enough for shallow frying when a smoky haze starts to float above the pan. Unlike butter and margarine, it contains no water, so one can fry or roast almost anything in it: it is ideal for pig-meats of any kind; it remains neutral, but will not give foods the flavour acquired with olive oil or butter, when either of these would be appropriate.

2. Lard is in a different category from dripping, the one fat being pure, the other not. (See dripping, p. 194.)

3. Alone, lard or a white cooking fat make feather-light pastry or scones, but neither will have any flavour – because neither fat has any flavour. This explains why lard and butter or margarine are so often used together in a recipe, the lightness given by the lard being complemented by the flavour of the other fat.

4. Lard or a white cooking fat are my first choice for greasing bread and cake tins, because things turn out eas-

ily. For large surfaces, melt the lard over low heat and brush it on. (The salt in butter and margarine, and their lower burning temperatures, means they are much less satisfactory.)

5. I like to use a little lard in bread, whether brown or white. I prefer the texture, besides finding that the bread keeps fresh longer. Not everyone agrees with me, though.

6. You can freeze pure lard for up to nine months, but why fill up the freezer with this? In a cool, dry place, a superior lard usually has a shelf life of three months, even longer in a refrigerator. (Melted and poured over certain dishes, lard is itself sometimes used as a preservative.)

## WHITE COOKING FATS

The best of these can be used at any time instead of lard and have a major advantage over most lards: they don't give off an unpleasant smell when heated in a frying pan. The best brands are 100% pure fat and, because virtually flavourless, odourless and colourless, are a good all-round substitute. (I think lard usually gives better results, however.)

Most brands are a blend of oils which may include animal, marine and vegetable sources, so, if you want a pure vegetable fat, be sure to read what's on the packet. All brands are fully refine, but the cheaper ones contain a higher proportion of cheaper oils, so one must not expect the same results from them. Some brands are slightly aerated and so easier to rub in than are traditional lards at an equally cold temperature.

The best cooking fats have a long shelf life even without refrigeration and, like liquid oils, do not congeal on fried or roast foods served cold – which may be an important consideration.

White cooking fats, like lard, are best for greasing bread and cake tins. Melt and brush them on, especially when greasing large surfaces like baking sheets. Dust cake tins with flour after greasing.

## DRIPPING

This is melted (rendered) fat from various sources, such as from suet, from a roast joint, from the fat under the skin of and inside a roast bird. After rendering, it must be strained finely to remove any tiny particles which might burn when you heat it.

Just as butter and olive oil are essential to the best cooks, so dripping is the undoing of many others. It is potentially the most impure fat one could use, and it can so easily spoil good food. The novice cook may tip any kind of fat, regardless of where it came from or what has been cooked in it, into a jar labelled 'dripping'. This horrible fat, possibly strong with age, is used (as I know from experience) in some households to fry or roast almost anything, even fish. Laden with impurities likely to irritate the most robust digestive system, it dominates the flavour of whatever is cooked in it unless first clarified.

Having said this, providing it is fresh, the appropriate dripping can be ideal for some dishes. Beef dripping is, by its nature, excellent for a beef stew or for roast beef and the potatoes to go with it; rendered lamb fat is quite all right to fry lamb chops, while chicken dripping has a delicate enough flavour to make it suitable for various chicken dishes – for instance to sweat the onions for a chicken casserole, or a vegetable soup, if you would rather use this than butter. Rendered chicken fat is particularly useful in Jewish cookery.

For deep-fat frying it is imperative to clarify dripping, otherwise the impurities in it burn at the high temperatures necessary to seal and cook the food, giving anything cooked in such fat a bitter taste and bad colour.

## SUET

This is the hard fat which surrounds and protects the kidneys. Even in ready-shredded packet form, when it has simply been clarified and mixed with a trace of flour to make it easier to handle as well as blend more easily with other ingredients, suet is one of the most natural fats with which we cook. In its fresh form, it is also one of the cheapest, but be sure it is fresh – hard and a good white colour, not soft or yellow. Beef suet is used rather than any other because it has the mildest flavour and adapts as well to sweet dishes as to savoury. I'm sure, for instance, that you would detect something strange about the taste of a jam roly-poly made with lamb suet, even if you couldn't identify what was wrong.

Always grate or shred fresh suet finely and cook both kinds of suet well, otherwise it will be indigestible. This is because suet needs a high temperature for melting to occur and if it is in lumps it takes longer still to melt. When baking, use a pre-heated hot oven; when steaming or boiling, have the water already boiling and allow time for long, slow cooking.

Although associated so much with long, slow cooking, suet can also form the basis of many dishes which will bake in half an hour (see below). Taking into account the short preparation time when using packet suet, you can get a suet-based main course to the table just as quickly as many others.

To store fresh suet, cover and refrigerate or freeze it, making sure there are no traces of blood on it. Keep packet suet in a cool, dry place. In extremely hot weather it may pay to refrigerate it, to prevent shreds of suet from sticking together. A highly purified and deodorised brand should keep for a year unopened, and for six months opened, though obviously the fresher any suet is when used, the better the end product. It is claimed that not only has a top-quality packet suet superior storing and eating qualities to fresh suet, but that a Christmas pudding made with it will have a better flavour and keep far longer than a pudding made with fresh suet.

## A few hints on cooking with suet

1. The normal rule of thumb is to use half suet to flour (self-raising) in pastry, half suet to breadcrumbs in stuffings. Although it has more limited uses than most other fats, there is none easier to mix in with other ingredients than packet suet: you need neither skill nor utensils, and the job is done in a few seconds.

2. For the best results, cook suet pastry as soon as possible after making.

3. When making shortcrust-type pastry, a lightly mixed egg used instead of some of the water makes a lighter, more crumbly pastry, especially suitable for eating cold. Use in the proportion of 1 egg to 250 g/8 oz self-raising flour. To make the pastry more flaky, sieve $1\frac{1}{2}$ level teaspoons of baking powder in with the flour and salt.

4. If you do not have, or are unable to eat suet, solid vegetable oil is often a good substitute. (See p. 189.)

## Uses for suet

1. Suetcrust pastry for savoury or sweet steamed or boiled puddings, e.g. steak and kidney pudding, grouse pudding, syrup pudding, jam or marmalade roly-poly, dumplings of various kinds.

2. Shortcrust-type pastry (baked suetcrust) to make savoury or sweet dishes, e.g. a meat or fruit pie, a kind of flan or quiche, Cornish pasties, sausage rolls, baked jam or marmalade roll, treacle tart. This is easy for anyone short of time or for those who are unable, for one reason or another, to rub fats in. Here is what you need.

| 250 g | 8 oz | self-raising flour seived together with |
|---|---|---|
| 1 level tsp salt | | |
| 125 g | 4 oz | packet suet |
| enough cold water to mix to a pliable dough | | |

3. Forcemeat balls, savoury pudding or stuffings to fill or accompany vegetables, fish, meat, poultry and/or game.

4. Christmas pudding, mincemeat, spotted dick, college pudding etc.

5. A crunchy topping for certain savoury or sweet dishes, e.g. beef and cheese crumble, a type of apple crumble.

6. Rendered down, to fry or roast, particularly any cut of beef.

## SATURATED AND POLYUNSATURATED FATS

Medical research has shown that many people who have suffered from heart attacks have a high level of certain types of fat in their bloodstream, including the fat-related substance, cholesterol, which is produced in the bodies of all animals, including man. Although cholesterol is essential to our bodies, we produce enough for our own purposes and so, strictly speaking, we do not need to *eat* any to stay healthy. However, as cholesterol is a normal animal product, all animal foods contain some. Egg yolk is a very rich source, but offal (e.g. liver and kidney), shellfish and dairy produce such as cream and butter also contain a lot of cholesterol. So does the hard fat round chops and joints.

In Western countries many people have fatty deposits on the inside wall of their arteries. These deposits build up over the years and make the channel of the artery progressively narrower. This can interfere with the blood supply to the heart and lead to a heart attack. A high level of cholesterol in the bloodstream may encourage the build-up of these deposits, thus increasing the risk of a heart attack. A heart attack occurs when the passage of blood through one of the arteries gets blocked, preventing the heart getting the oxygen it needs. Often, the blockage is caused by the formation of a blood clot. Blood clots seem more likely to form if the artery is already clogged up. The larger the artery which gets blocked, the more likely it is that the heart attack will be serious, even fatal. Although a heart attack can occur quite suddenly and without warning, the underlying disease in the arteries may have been developing for many years.

Many doctors and scientists agree that the *kind* of fat we use is very important. On a long-term basis, the cholesterol level in the blood can be lowered by avoiding foods high in saturated fatty acids and using foods high in polyunsaturated fatty acids instead. All the different fats found in foods contain fatty acids, which are of two main types.

**Saturated fats** – those which contain a high proportion of saturated fatty acids. *They are usually hard or solid at room temperature.* Foods of animal origin and some other foods (such as certain vegetable oils which solidify when refrigerated, e.g. coconut oil) contain mainly saturated fats. All hard (packet) margarines contain saturated fats; in fact the very process of hardening the fat in the manufacture of margarine from vegetable oils involves the saturation of a proportion of the fat. The physical and chemical changes taking place during hardening mean that the fatty acids are converted to the saturated form.

**Polyunsaturated fats** – those which contain a high proportion of polyunsaturated fatty acids and which are *very soft or even liquid at room temperature.* They are often called oils rather than fats. These are found naturally in many seeds and nuts, or in products made from these, e.g. corn oil, sunflower oil. Polyunsaturated fat is usually of plant origin.

Margarines and oils which contain a high proportion of polyunsaturated fats are clearly labelled.

Olive oil and groundnut oil are *mono-unsaturated fats.* They are regarded as neutral in terms of coronary heart disease, i.e. neither harmful nor beneficial.

The type of fat eaten will not affect the body weight in any way as all fats and oils, whether of the saturated or the polyunsaturated kind, have the same calorie content.

To see at a glance which fats are which, see the fat guide below.

## Fat guide for those with heart problems

| Fats high in saturated fat | Fats high in unsaturated fat |
|---|---|
| butter | *sunflower oil margarines |
| lard | oils, *corn |
| white cooking fats | *cotton seed |
| dripping | groundnut |
| all hard margarines | olive |
| most soft margarines | *safflower |
| oils, coconut | *sesame |
|     solid | *soya |
| suet | *sunflower |
| cream | *walnut |

*high in *poly*unsaturated fat

*With acknowledgements, in alphabetical order, to:*

berry Bros & Rudd Ltd, Wine and Spirit Merchants, re olive oils
The Butter Information Council
CPC (United Kingdom) Ltd, makers of Mazola (Uncle Toby) corn
   oil
Paul Winner Marketing Communications Ltd
The Pura Lard Group, makers of Pura soft lard and Pura solid
   vegetable oil
RHM Foods Ltd, makers of Atora suet
Van den Berghs, makers of (amongst other fats) Flora oil; Flora,
   Stork, Echo, Blue Band and Krona margarines; Spry and
   Cookeen; Outline low fat spread
Leslie Zyw, article on olive oil

# Soufflés

## ANNE WILLAN

I have always been fascinated by soufflés: their nonchalant transformation in the oven to a towering golden puff, their receptiveness to almost any flavour and their challenge not only to the cook's skill, but also to his imagination. For the carefree appearance of the perfect soufflé is backed by hard technical expertise and by an instinctive flair. Like counterpoint music, it presents an intriguing, almost mathematical balance of opposing forces (once upon a time, I was a very elementary mathematician).

Essentially, a soufflé consists of two contrasting parts: whipped egg whites and a base to give flavour. More egg whites give a lighter soufflé, fewer egg whites mean the soufflé has more taste. The next decision is posed by thickening: a binding agent such as flour stabilises the basic mixture, but also weighs it down, so that the flourless soufflé holds a tantalising fascination. Another dilemma is oven temperature, which can ascend to the very hot, when the soufflé puffs spectacularly but drops with sometimes dizzy speed, or towards moderate, when the mixture cooks gently and thoroughly but without the surprise of a soft, creamy centre. Even the soufflé dish offers a choice, for in a deep dish the soufflé rises higher but is more likely to crack and spill at the sides. Happily all these hazards are controllable. Making soufflés is a risk, but a calculated one, a gamble which I must say I relish every time.

I'm not the only one. For centuries master chefs have been assessing the odds and trying to reduce the risks inherent in cooking a soufflé. The capacity of egg whites to expand and lighten a mixture was recognised by the Italian cooks of the Renaissance, possibly following the example of painters who mixed their tempera colours with egg white. (Italian *sformati* and certain types of *budini*, aerated puddings that are baked and unmoulded, may be ancestors of the soufflé.) The whisk is depicted in kitchen scenes of the 1500s, so its value for beating egg whites for extra lightness was almost certainly appreciated.

Its partner, the copper bowl, does not appear until centuries later. To me it is the indispensable adjunct to the successful soufflé – when whisked in a copper bowl with a balloon whisk, egg whites acquire a volume and density of texture that is almost impossible to duplicate by any other means. Granted, not everyone agrees with me and, in any case, no modern restaurant can afford the elbow grease involved. I must admit that a heavy-duty electric beater with a metal bowl produces good results if a pinch of salt or cream of tartar is added. For sweet soufflés a tablespoon or two of sugar whisked in when the whites are stiff makes a meringue which holds up much better than the plain whites.

From renaissance Italy, the action moved to France. Writing in 1651, the Sieur de la Varenne, cook to the Marquis d'Uxelles ( of *duxelles* fame), describes *oeufs à la neige* in which the principles of the modern soufflé are in evidence. He makes a sweet white sauce with milk, sugar, plain egg whites (or yolks) and flour, then folds in whipped egg whites. The actual word 'soufflé' does not appear until nearly a century later, the first mention I've found being in 1749 with Menon's *crème de ris soufflée*. This resembles La Varenne's recipe in method, but orange flower water is added as flavouring, and purée of rice is used instead of flour for thickening.

By this date, the question of thickening, particularly of sauces, preoccupied cooks. Potato starch, breadcrumbs, rice and flour were all used, with rice the favourite for soufflés.

Nowadays flour is the most common, in the guise of *béchamel* or *velouté* sauce (for savoury soufflés) and pastry cream (for sweet). Much depends on the amount used, but a flour-thickened soufflé can be slightly solid and the nineteenth century food authority Joseph Favre complained of 'an unpleasant taste of dough'. Rice, by contrast, is so much out of fashion that I tried it only recently; the results were excellent, though the basic purée took an hour to cook.

Breadcrumbs are lighter than flour or rice, but absorb less liquid and therefore hold less firmly. My favourite thickening for delicate soufflés is potato starch ( or if not, arrowroot), but the soufflé has a disconcerting tendency to thin suddenly if overcooked or left to stand – I've had more than one last minute panic with a mixture turned suddenly runny in the pan. Egg whites can also be used for thickening, and the latest idea for hot soufflés is, surprisingly, gelatine, suggested by the *cuisine minceur* chef, Michel Guérard. The gelatine acts rather like meatless meat glaze and personally I think the mixture tends to be glued rather than thickened.

The ultimate perfection of the flourless soufflé has long preoccupied the inventive cook. Certain ingredients like chocolate bind by themselves. Cooking methods can circumvent the problem – I've made a delicious lemon soufflé based on lemon curd, for instance; thick stewed apples or pears also make an acceptable base. The majority of ingredients, however, do not stick together by nature. An egg custard cannot be used as a base for a sweet soufflé, for example, because it is too sloppy to mix smoothly into whipped egg whites, and minced meat or shellfish is too dry, leading to a granular texture. The American cook Julia Child once tried 39 different ways of making a fresh strawberry soufflé without flour, but with no success. In the oven, fresh strawberries produce quantities of juice; her reluctant conclusion was they must either be mixed with a thickener (such as pastry cream) or thoroughly cooked to a pulp, thus losing their fresh flavour.

Proportions for a soufflé are also a matter of debate. Until the end of the nineteenth century, an equal number of whites and yolks was normally used, leading to a firm soufflé almost resembling today's *mousseline.* Escoffier, writing in 1902, adds one or two extra whites to his soufflés. I like to go further and use half as much again, leading to proportions like three egg yolks to five egg whites, four yolks to six whites, five to eight and so on. Of course, yolks can be omitted altogether, but the soufflé tends to be dry and anaemic. The proportion of egg whites to basic mixture is more predictable. Most cooks like to add three or four times the volume of whipped egg whites, increasing egg whites slightly if the basic mixture is piquant, or reducing them for a firmer texture.

Eggs and thickening are but the foundation of a soufflé; its real character comes from key ingredients like fish, meat, poultry and vegetables for a savoury soufflé; or nuts, fruits and liqueurs, favourites for a dessert soufflé. The more forceful the flavour to balance the bland egg whites, the better: cheese, mushrooms, spinach, chocolate and lemon are outstanding, with game and ham among the best of meats, and lobster or crab the best of shellfish. Milder flavours need assistance – fish is often pepped up with curry, vegetables with cheese and orange with Grand Marnier.

The cooks of yesteryear were more adventurous. I'd love to try an anise and caramel soufflé, dating from 1815 (Carême), or a green coffee soufflé of 1846 (Soyer), if only they were practicable today. (Until the 1850s, almost all soufflé recipes were sweet, and even now sweet recipes outnumber savoury ones in the average cookbook.) However, modern chefs have been trying offbeat combinations like the *soufflé d'oranges sanguines et citrons verts* (blood oranges and lime) and the *soufflé d'oursins* (sea urchins) I have tasted recently at *nouvelle cuisine* restaurants. Soufflés are, of course, a worthy end for left-overs; one of the best soufflés I ever made was based on *ratatouille*, chopped and cooked until very stiff before the egg whites were folded in.

Soufflé dishes are a story in themselves. The modern straight-sided china dish is modelled on a *timbale*, a high-sided container whose name derives from *at-tabl*, the Arab for drum. *Timbales* were made of metal or china (or simply of pastry dough), and all were used for soufflés. In fact the words of the eighteenth century chef Vincent la Chapelle, 'you can shape your *gâteau de riz* (soufflé) in any mould you think suitable', still hold today, and charlotte moulds, entrée dishes and even saucepans can be pressed into service.

They do not all give quite the same results. In a metal dish the heat penetrates at once so the soufflé cooks more quickly, but also falls more rapidly. Softer mixtures should not be cooked in a tall mould as they tend to collapse at the sides, as do very large soufflés. Middle-sized soufflés to serve three or four people are most practical – attractive though individual soufflés are, they fall too fast. Not all soufflé-type mixtures are necessarily moulded; they may be cooked as *roulades* (rolled with a filling like a savoury Swiss roll), or sufficient egg whites may be added to a pudding or fritter to earn it the name 'soufflé'. Cold soufflés are even more of a cheat, for despite their appearance they have not risen at all, but are set with gelatine or frozen inside a paper collar so they give the impression – a charming one – of having risen.

For many years true soufflés were baked in their dishes enclosed by a covered casserole for protection from direct heat – Carême describes their use in detail. Late nineteenth century chefs, including Escoffier, advised wrapping a collar around the dish both to support the mixture and to protect it. However, none of the French chefs I've worked with finds this necessary. They fill the dish to within 1 cm/½ inch of the brim, smoothing the mixture carefully and loosening it from the rim with a twist of the thumb. They also take immense pains in buttering the sides of the dish – some like to freeze it, then butter it a second time. The smallest sticking point will make the soufflé tilt and bubble over in the oven. Uneven oven heat will do the same damage, so a constant eye must be kept to check that the soufflé is rising vertically.

The so-called soufflés of the eighteenth century resembled puddings, of necessity resilient to all kinds of buffeting. In many ways it is Carême who was the inventor of the modern soufflé, for his career coincided with the development of the closed draught oven which made accurate heat control possible. Since then, soufflés have become progressively lighter, thanks to the thermostat, for temperature control, and above all, quick and easy change in the speed of cooking, is vital to all delicate cuisine. The actual temperature at which a soufflé cooks is much less important – a good mixture that has been properly folded with plenty of air will rise sooner or later in almost any oven.

In present-day cookbooks, suggested temperatures range from gas 2/150°C/300°F to gas 9/240°C/475°F. I always incline to a hot oven, mainly because the soufflé cooks quickly enough for me to await the last guest before putting the dish in the oven. High heat gives the soufflé a crisp outside and a soft centre which acts as a kind of sauce, ideal for sweet soufflés and plain flavours like cheese. However, fish, meat and vegetable soufflés based on a heavy purée do better at a lower temperature so that they cook through to the centre.

A soufflé is done when it is puffed and brown, that much is obvious. But some mixtures rise more than others, so when it looks ready I like to give the soufflé a trial shake (like babies, soufflés prefer a firm hand). The mixture should be firm on the outside and sloppy or firm in the centre, depending on the consistency wanted. Signs of overcooking are shrunken sides and a convex top, showing the centre of the soufflé is very hot. The alarm must be sounded at once, for an overdone soufflé is sad indeed, wrinkled, shrunk and so tough that it resists the serving spoon.

The cooking of a soufflé can be slowed by lowering the oven temperature (for speed, stick a spoon in the door to let out hot air), but when cooked it must be served immediately. 'Summon the *maître d'hôtel*,' urges Carême, 'and dispatch him to the dining room at once.' The crusty old chef who taught me in Paris twenty years ago did his best to circumvent this injunction. When his soufflé was ready, he would leave the oven door wide open and after two or three minutes, when the cooler side of the soufflé fell, he would give the dish a half turn so that the fallen half puffed again inside the warm oven and the other half subsided. This went on for 15 or 20 minutes, until shutting the door for a few seconds, he would reveal the soufflé puffed as good as new as if he were a conjuror. Unfortunately, as with all conjuring tricks, there was a catch – the soufflé was so laden with flour that it was almost inedible.

The right moment for a soufflé to wait is before, not after, baking. There's never any problem making the basic mixture several hours ahead and, contrary to the advice given in most cookbooks, I've discovered that the finished soufflé can wait to be baked. By trial and surprisingly little error at La Varenne cooking school in Paris, we've found that a well mixed soufflé can be kept in the refrigerator an hour or two before baking with no trouble at all, even if it contains no flour. One luckless soufflé was forgotten for 36 hours, yet it emerged from the oven without a trace of its ordeal.

The speed with which a soufflé must be served leaves no time for fancy decorations. Escoffier is succinct: 'the decoration of soufflés is optional and, in any case, must be sober'. In the old days, a sweet soufflé would be glazed with caramel using a red-hot iron from the open fire, but now this is replaced by a sprinkling of icing sugar. A few thin slices of orange or strawberry may be laid somewhat precariously on top of a sweet soufflé, but savoury ones are left plain. And what more splendid sight could there be than a lofty soufflé, mushrooming over its pretty dish, set in classic style on a damask napkin on a silver tray? From texture to taste to style of presentation it sums up 400 years of experiment by master chefs – gamblers to a man.

## Soufflé de carottes futuriste
## (carrot soufflé)

This contemporary soufflé, typical of *nouvelle cuisine*, has been reduced to the bare essentials – unthickened carrot purée and whipped egg whites.

| 750 g | 1½ lb | carrots, sliced |
|---|---|---|
| 15 g | ½ oz | crystallised ginger |
| 30 g | 1 oz | butter |
| 3 egg yolks | | |
| salt, pepper | | |
| ½ tsp sugar (optional) | | |
| 5 egg whites | | |
| Soufflé dish (1½ litre/3 pint capacity) | | |
| Serves 4 | | |

Put the carrots in cold salted water, bring to a boil and simmer 10–15 minutes or until very tender. Soak ginger in hot water for 5 minutes to dissolve sugar, then drain and chop it. Drain the carrots thoroughly and purée in a blender or food mill. Melt the butter in a saucepan, add the carrot purée and cook gently, stirring, until it is dry and draws away from the sides of the pan. Take from the heat and beat in the egg yolks. Heat gently for half a minute until the purée thickens slightly. Stir in the ginger and taste – season with salt, pepper and sugar as necessary; the purée should be highly seasoned. It can be prepared 3–4 hours ahead and kept covered in the refrigerator.

To finish: butter the soufflé dish and set the oven at very hot (gas 7/220°C/425°F). Gently heat the carrot purée.

Whip the egg whites, adding a pinch of salt to help them stiffen. Fold a quarter of the egg whites into the warm carrot purée, add this mixture back to the remaining egg whites and fold together as lightly as possible. Transfer to the prepared soufflé dish and bake in the oven 12–15 minutes or until the soufflé is puffed and brown, but still soft in the centre. Serve at once. If overcooked the soufflé is very dry.

## Soufflé de saumon Ali-Bab
## (Salmon soufflé Ali-Bab)

Ali-Bab is the pseudonym of D. Henri Babinski who wrote a brilliant if eccentric *Livre de Cuisine* in 1912 (recently reprinted). Personally, if I'm looking for a new soufflé, I turn to Ali-Bab, and this salmon mixture, which is almost a *mousseline*, is typical of his inventiveness. The base is thickened only with egg whites, without any yolks for richness, and the soufflé is cooked slowly in a water-bath giving it a close, firm texture. Babinski suggests the same method for lobster, crab and game. Strictly speaking, the raw meat or fish should be forced through an old-fashioned drum sieve, but a blender or food processor give just as good results.

| | | |
|---|---|---|
| 1 kg | 2 lb | *piece of raw salmon* |
| 6 egg whites | | |
| 300 ml | ½ pint | *double cream* |
| salt, pepper | | |
| sauce blanche au beurre (*below*) | | |
| Soufflé dish (1½ litre/3 pint capacity) | | |
| Serves 8 | | |

Remove skin and all bones from the salmon (reserve them for sauce) and cut the flesh in pieces – there should be 600 g/1¼ lb meat. Whip 2 egg whites until frothy. In a blender work a tablespoon of the salmon to a purée with a tablespoon of the cream and half a tablespoon of whipped egg white. Turn into a bowl and repeat until all the salmon, cream and whipped egg whites are used. In a food processor the mixture can be worked in larger quantities. Set the bowl of salmon mixture over ice and beat in salt and pepper to taste. The mixture can be prepared ahead and kept over ice or in the refrigerator for up to 4 hours.

To finish: butter the soufflé dish and set the oven at moderate (gas 4/180° C/350° F). Bring a water-bath to a boil on top of the stove. Stiffly whip the remaining egg whites, adding a pinch of salt to help them stiffen. Fold a quarter of the egg whites into the iced salmon mixture, then add this mixture back to the remaining egg whites and fold together as lightly as possible. Transfer to the prepared soufflé dish and set it in the water-bath. Bring it to a boil on top of the stove, then bake in the water-bath in the heated oven 50–60 minutes or until the soufflé is brown and firm in the centre. Serve it at once with the butter sauce separately.

## Sauce blanche au beurre

(White butter sauce for fish)

Ali-Bab suggests serving a shrimp sauce with salmon soufflé, and a few baby shrimps can be added to this version of *hollandaise* sauce.

| | | |
|---|---|---|
| bones from the salmon (above) | | |
| ½ onion, sliced | | |
| bouquet garni | | |
| ½ tsp peppercorns | | |
| 185 ml | 6 fl oz | white wine |
| 185 ml | 6 fl oz | water |
| 250 g | ½ lb | butter |
| 2 egg yolks | | |
| salt, white pepper | | |
| Makes a scant 250 ml/½ pint sauce | | |

In a saucepan (not aluminium) put the fish bones, onion, bouquet garni, peppercorns, wine and water. Bring to a boil, skim and simmer 20 minutes. Let this fish stock cool. Strain it into a heavy-based saucepan and boil until reduced to 2 tablespoons. Melt the butter and leave to cool. Let the reduced fish stock cool until tepid, then whisk in the egg yolks. Whisk over low heat 2–3 minutes until the mixture forms a mousse thick enough to leave a ribbon trail when the whisk is lifted. Take from the heat and whisk in the melted butter a tablespoon at a time. Do not add the milky whey at the bottom of the butter. If the butter is added too quickly, the sauce will curdle. Add salt and pepper and taste for seasoning. The sauce can be kept warm in a water-bath at the side of the stove for 15–30 minutes, but if it gets hotter than hand-hot, it will curdle.

## Soufflé à la royale Escoffier

(Candied fruit soufflé with kirsch)

Soufflés were an Escoffier favourite – spectacular, light on a jaded digestion and easily transformed by a different flavouring to a 'new' creation on which he could bestow a chic title. This particular vanilla soufflé features lady-fingers and candied fruits soaked in kirsch. The flavour of the soufflé depends largely on the quality of the candied fruits – supermarket cherries will not do.

| 150 g | 5 oz | chopped mixed candied fruit |
|---|---|---|
| 60 ml | 2 fl oz | kirsch |
| 4 lady-fingers | | |
| 185 ml | 6 fl oz | milk |
| 1 vanilla bean, split | | |
| 60 g | 2 oz | sugar |
| 20 g | ⅔ oz | flour mixed to a paste with 60 ml /2 fl oz milk |

| 15 g | ½ oz | butter |
|---|---|---|
| 4 egg yolks | | |
| 6 egg whites | | |
| icing sugar for sprinkling | | |
| Soufflé dish (1½ litre/3 pint capacity) | | |
| Serves 4 to 6 | | |

Wash and finely chop the candied fruit. Add 1 tablespoon kirsch, cover and leave to macerate at least 1 hour. Roughly chop lady-fingers, sprinkle with remaining kirsch and cover. For the soufflé base: scald the milk with the vanilla bean, cover and leave to infuse over low heat 10–15 minutes. Stir in all but 2 tablespoons of the sugar until dissolved, then add the paste of flour. Bring to a boil, stirring constantly until the mixture thickens; simmer 2 minutes. Take from the heat and discard the vanilla bean. Dot the top of the mixture with butter and let cool. The butter will melt and prevent a skin forming. The soufflé can be prepared 2–3 hours ahead to this point.

To finish: butter the soufflé dish and set the oven at moderately hot (gas 5/190° C/375° F). Heat the vanilla mixture, beat in the egg yolks and cook until the mixture thickens slightly. Take from the heat and beat in the macerated fruits, making sure they do not stick together; keep warm. Whip the egg whites, add the reserved sugar and continue beating 30 seconds to make a light meringue. Fold a quarter of this meringue into the warm fruit and vanilla mixture, add this back to the remaining egg whites and fold together as lightly as possible. Spoon a third of the mixture into the prepared soufflé dish, lay half the lady-fingers on top. Add half the remaining soufflé mixture and cover with the remaining lady-fingers followed by the rest of the soufflé mixture. Smooth the top and bake the soufflé in the oven 20–25 minutes until puffed and brown but still soft in the centre. Sprinkle with icing sugar and serve at once.

## Soufflé à la menthe de Carême
(Carême's mint soufflé)

The purée of rice used here by Carême dates back to the first soufflés and continued as the preferred thickening right through the nineteenth century until Escoffier. The rice gives a light texture with an agreeable background taste. Carême suggests some interesting flavours for the rice base – toasted orange flowers, rum punch, bitter almonds, a mixture of four citrus fruits and this fresh mint soufflé. Proportions of the original recipe have been changed to give a lighter soufflé more familiar to today's tastes.

| | | |
|---|---|---|
| 60 g | 2 oz | *roundp-grain rice* |
| 600 ml | 1 pint | *milk* |
| 60 g | 2 oz | *sugar* |
| 30 g | 1 oz | *butter* |
| 6 tbs chopped fresh mint | | |
| grated rind of 2 lemons | | |
| 6 eggs separated | | |
| icing sugar for sprinkling | | |
| Soufflé dish (2½ litre/4½ pint capacity) | | |
| Serves 6 to 8 | | |

To make the rice purée: in a heavy-based pan put the rice with plenty of water, bring to a boil and simmer 5 minutes. Drain, return the rice to the pan with two thirds of the milk and cover. Simmer 45–60 minutes or until the rice is very soft when crushed between the fingers. (The rice sticks easily and is best cooked in a water-bath.) Add all but 2 tablespoons of the sugar and continue cooking 10 minutes. The milk should have reduced by about half, but if not take off the lid and boil it, stirring, until evaporated. Stir in the butter and purée the rice mixture in a blender or with a food mill; there should be 350 ml/12 fl oz purée.

For the soufflé base: scald the remaining milk, add the mint and lemon rind, cover and leave to infuse over low heat 10–15 minutes. Strain the milk and stir it into the rice purée. Bring the mixture to a boil. Take from the heat and beat in the egg yolks, one by one; they will cook in the heat of the mixture and thicken it slightly. The soufflé base can be prepared 3–4 hours ahead and kept covered in the refrigerator.

To finish: butter the soufflé dish and set the oven at moderately hot (gas 5/190° C/375° F). Gently heat the rice mixture. Stiffly whip the egg whites, add the reserved sugar and continue beating 30 seconds to make a light meringue. Stir a quarter of this meringue into the soufflé base, add the mixture back to the remaining egg whites and fold together as lightly as possible. Transfer the mixture to the soufflé dish, smooth the top and bake in the heated oven 40–45 minutes or until puffed and brown. Sprinkle with icing sugar and serve at once.

## Soufflé d'endive Joseph Favre
(Chicory soufflé)

In his monumental dictionary published in 1883, chef Joseph Favre explores ingredients and techniques from the viewpoint of the professional cook. He is particularly thorough on soufflés, suggesting tricks like adding whole eggs to the basic mixture to help thicken it. For vegetable soufflés like this one, he advises adding cheese.

| 15 g | ½ oz | butter |
|---|---|---|
| 250 g | ½ lb | chicory, sliced |
| 300 ml | ½ pint | single cream |
| salt, pepper and ground nutmeg | | |
| béchamel sauce (below) | | |
| 8 eggs | | |
| 60 g | 2 oz | grated gruyère cheese |
| Soufflé dish (2½ litre/4½ pint capacity) | | |
| Serves 6 | | |

In a saucepan melt the butter, add the chicory with cream, salt, pepper and nutmeg. Cover and cook gently 10–15 minutes until very tender, stirring occasionally. Purée the mixture in a blender or food processor. Return it to the heat and cook to dry and thicken, stirring constantly; it should fall easily from the spoon. Make the *béchamel* sauce and beat in the purée. Whisk in 2 whole eggs and 4 egg yolks and cook gently, stirring, until the mixture thickens slightly. Take it from the heat. The basic mixture can be prepared 3–4 hours ahead up to this point; keep it covered in the refrigerator.

To finish: butter the soufflé dish and set the oven at hot (gas 6/200° C/400° F). Gently heat the basic mixture, stir in all but 2 tablespoons of the cheese and taste for seasoning – it should be quite peppery. Stiffly whip remaining 6 egg whites, adding a pinch of salt to help them stiffen. Stir a quarter of the egg whites into the warm mixture, then add this mixture back to the remaining egg whites. Fold together as lightly as possible, transfer to the prepared soufflé dish and sprinkle with the remaining cheese. Bake in the heated oven for 20–25 minutes or until the soufflé is puffed and brown. Serve at once.

## Sauce Béchamel (Béchamel sauce)

| 185 ml | 6 fl oz | milk |
|--------|---------|------|
| 1 slice of onion | | |
| 1 bay leaf | | |
| 6 peppercorns | | |
| 30 g | 1 oz | butter |
| 30 g | 1 oz | flour |

*Makes 185 ml/6 fl oz sauce*

Scald the milk in a saucepan. Add the onion, bay leaf and peppercorns, cover and leave in a warm place 5–10 minutes.

Meanwhile make the roux: in a heavy-bottomed saucepan melt the butter, whisk in the flour and cook 1–2 minutes until the roux is foaming but not browned; let it cool. Strain in the hot milk, whisking, then bring the sauce to a boil, whisking constantly. Simmer 3–5 minutes. If the sauce is not used at once, rub the surface with butter to prevent a skin from forming.

*Sources:*

Carême, Antonin: *Le Pâtissier Royal*, Paris 1815.

Escoffier, Auguste: *Le Guide Culinaire*, Paris 1902. Revised and reprinted in English and French.

La Chapelle, Vincent: *The Modern Cook*, London 1733.

La Varenne: *Le Cuisinier François*, Paris 1651. Reprint of 1696 edition available from Daniel Morcrette, 95270 Luzarches, France.

Menon: *La Science du Maître d'Hôtel Cuisinier*, Paris 1749.

Soyer, Alexis: *The Gastronomic Regenerator*, London 1846.

Favre, Joseph: *Dictionnaire Universel de Cuisine Pratique*, Paris 1833 (4 volumes).

# Index